THE PICTORIAL GUIDE
(pages 1 - 168)

SYMBOLS and ABBREVIATIONS

IN THE DETAILED ROUTE MAPS:

Map Scale: 2" = 1 mile   *North is top of the page*

Route on motor road   *Unenclosed* ≈≈≈≈ *Enclosed* ≈≈≈≈

Good footpath
(sufficiently distinct to be followed in mist)

Intermittent footpath
(difficult to follow in mist)

No path; route recommended

Wall ∞∞∞∞∞∞∞∞   Broken wall ∘∘∘∘∘∘∘∘∘∘∘

Fence ┼┼┼┼┼┼┼┼┼   Broken fence ᴵᴵᴵᴵᴵᴵᴵᴵᴵᴵᴵᴵᴵ

Marshy ground ⋎⋎⋎⋎⋎⋎   Trees ♧♧♧♧♧♧

Crags ᵐᵐᵐᵐ   Scree ░░░   Boulders ◌◌◌◌

Stream or River ∿∿∿
(arrow indicates direction of flow)

Waterfall ∿—∿   Bridge ∿═∿

Buildings ▪▪▫▪   Unenclosed road ⋯⋯⋯⋯

Summit cairn ▲   Other (prominent) cairns △ △

Ordnance column ⌂   Limestone clints ⁴⁄₁ ⁴⁄₁ ⁴⁄₁ ᴴ⁴⁄₁

Contours (at 100' intervals) ⋯1400⋯   Railway ━━━━

Map continuation ⤙‖127   Abbreviations:
(page number)   O.S: Ordnance Survey
                                             Y.H: Youth Hostel
Miles from St. Bees ⟨72⟩
(on main route only)

IN THE SECTION MAPS:

Map Scale: ¼" = 1 mile

Beeline (St. Bees Head to Ro...

D0425648

THE PICTORIAL GUIDES
TO THE
LAKELAND FELLS

A COAST TO COAST WALK

—————— **REVISED EDITION** ——————

View from South Head, St. Bees, looking to Black Combe

A COAST TO COAST WALK

(ST. BEES HEAD to ROBIN HOOD'S BAY)

A PICTORIAL GUIDE

AWainwright

1973

PUBLISHED
by
MICHAEL JOSEPH
LONDON

MICHAEL JOSEPH LTD

Published by the Penguin Group
27 Wrights Lane, London W8, England

Penguin Books Ltd Registered Offices:
Harmondsworth, Middlesex, England

First published by Michael Joseph 1992
Revised edition 1994
Second impression (with minor changes) November 1995
Third impression (with minor changes) February 1998

Originally published by the Westmorland Gazette, 1973

© 1992, 1994, 1995, 1998 Michael Joseph Ltd

Printed by Clays Ltd, Bungay

ISBN O 7181 4072 9

Dedicated to

THE SECOND PERSON
(unidentifiable as yet)
**TO WALK FROM
ST. BEES HEAD
TO ROBIN HOOD'S BAY**

PUBLISHER'S NOTE: When A. Wainwright planned his unique cross-England expedition over twenty-five years ago, he chose a route which, as he says in his Introduction on page iii, he hoped would commit no act of trespass or offence against privacy. It later transpired that certain sections of the route did indeed cross land over which there was no public right of way, and this revised edition sets out to amend those sections so that the walk is now either on public roads, public rights of way, or on permissive paths.

Wainwright text which covers parts of the route which are no longer valid has been clearly marked with a bold line in the left- or right-hand margins. An asterisk then leads to the new typeset copy describing the revised route which appears, in the main, at the foot of the affected pages. Walkers should, therefore, always refer to the new text whenever original copy marked with a bold line is reached. On occasion, the map has been very slightly amended but no revised text required.

The publisher would like to thank the following organisations who have given much valuable time and help in assisting them to produce this revised route:

The Forestry Commission (Lakes Forest District); The Lake District National Park Authority; The National Trust (North West Region); The East Cumbria Countryside Project; The Yorkshire Dales National Park Authority; and the North York Moors National Park Authority. Especial thanks should also go to all the landowners who have given permission for the Coast to Coast Walk to cross their private land on permissive or concessionary paths.

Finally, we must acknowledge the debt due to Chris Jesty who has, with the approval of the Wainwright Estate, amended most sympathetically the Wainwright maps where necessary, as well as checking the route on the ground. The book has been revised for changes of route, but not for minor changes such as the removal of fences.

CONTENTS

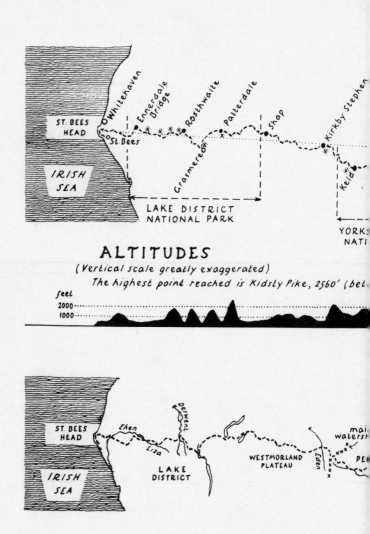

ALTITUDES
(Vertical scale greatly exaggerated)
The highest point reached is Kidsty Pike, 2560' (bel

THE ROUTE

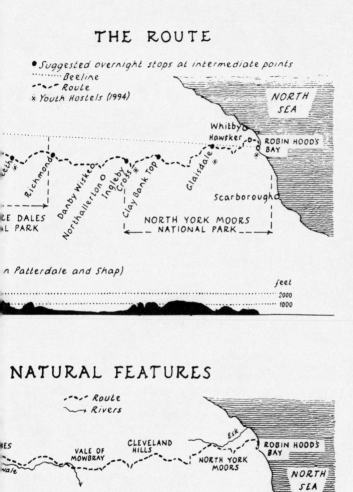

- Suggested overnight stops at intermediate points
.... Beeline
--.-- Route
x Youth Hostels (1994)

NORTH SEA

Whitby
Hawsker
ROBIN HOOD'S BAY

Richmond
Danby Wiske
Northallerton
Ingleby Cross
Clay Bank Top
Glaisdale
Scarborough

E DALES
L PARK

NORTH YORK MOORS
NATIONAL PARK

n Patterdale and Shap)

feet
2000
1000

NATURAL FEATURES

--.-- Route
⌒⌒ Rivers

Esk

VALE OF MOWBRAY
CLEVELAND HILLS
NORTH YORK MOORS
ROBIN HOOD'S BAY

NORTH SEA

ale

Top map slightly amended 1994

St. Bees Head

INTRODUCTION

Every walker who plans a cross-country expedition refers to his maps, looks for the footpaths and the bridleways and the areas of open access, links them together by quiet roads and lanes that avoid towns and busy traffic arteries, and so devises a pleasant route to his objective that he is free to walk, as is any man, without fear of trespass or restriction.

This is precisely what I have done in the book. To the best of my knowledge the route described will commit no offence against privacy nor trample on the sensitive corns of landowners and tenants. It is a country walk of the sort that enthusiasts for the hills and open spaces indulge in every weekend. It's a bit longer than most, that's all.

The point I want to emphasise is that the route herein described is in no sense an "official route" such as the Pennine Way — it has not needed the approval of the Countryside Commission or indeed any other body nor have any permissions needed to be sought. It is a harmless and enjoyable walk across England, entirely (so far as I am aware) on existing rights of way or over ground where access is traditionally free to all.

The walk is one I have long had in mind, and in 1972 finally accomplished; and I have committed it to print partly because the growing popularity of the Pennine Way indicates that many people of all ages welcome the challenge of a long-distance walk, and partly because I want to encourage in others the ambition to devise with the aid of maps their own cross-country marathons and not be merely followers of other people's routes: there is no end to the possibilities for originality and initiative. And partly, I suppose, because I like to write about my walks and by doing so live them over again.

Pillar,
Lake District

One should always have a definite objective, in a walk as in life — it is so much more satisfying to reach a target by personal effort than to wander aimlessly. An objective is an ambition, and life without ambition is ..... well, aimless wandering.
The objective in this book is Robin Hood's Bay, on the Yorkshire coast: doubly satisfying because it is not only an attractive place to finish a walk (ice cream, girls and all that — oh, and scenery) but also very definitive: here land ends and sea begins. You can't walk on water, and Robin Hood's Bay is a definite full stop, a terminus absolute.

The route follows an approximate beeline (if a beeline can ever be approximate!) from one side of England to the other: from St. Bees Head on the Irish Sea to Robin Hood's Bay on the North Sea and if a ruler is placed across a map between these two points it will be seen at a glance that the grandest territory in the north of England is traversed by it; indeed, two-thirds of the route lies through the areas of three National Parks.

The walk commences on the sea-cliffs of St. Bees Head, passes through the heart of Lakeland, and crosses the Westmorland limestone plateau, the Eden Valley and the Pennine watershed, whence it accompanies Swaledale and then aims across the Vale of Mowbray to the Cleveland Hills and North York Moors to end on the sea-cliffs of Robin Hood's Bay.

Surely there cannot be a finer itinerary for a long-distance walk! For sustained beauty, variety and interest it puts the Pennine Way to shame.

On the
Cleveland
Hills

It is never possible to follow a dead-straight beeline over a long distance without trespassing: climbing fences, wading rivers, perhaps swimming sheets of water, and walking through houses and gardens. In fact, no straight line on a map will give a dead-straight beeline because it is now generally accepted in the best circles that the earth is round, not flat, and a straight line on a map must therefore be incorrect to the extent of the curvature between the two points, however slight. The route given in this book makes no attempt to follow a straight line: deviations are necessary throughout, primarily to avoid private ground but additionally to take the opportunity of visiting places of special interest nearby — without ever losing sight of the final objective. Thus although the straight line gives a mileage of 125, the route mileage is 190 : half as far again.

The Old Gang Mines
near Swaledale

The countryside traversed is beautiful almost everywhere, yet extremely varied in character, with mountains and hills, valleys and rivers, heather moors and sea cliffs combining in a pageant of colourful scenery. It is of great interest both topographically and geologically, the structure of the terrain and the formations of the rocks showing marked changes from one district to the next. Evidences in plenty are met of prehistoric and early British settlements, while many abandoned mineral workings dating from medieval times offer a fascinating study for the industrial archaeologist. You see part of the history of England on this walk.

The route, which has a bias in favour of high ground rather than low, is divided into convenient sections, each of sufficient distance to provide a good day's march for the average walker and ending at a place where overnight lodgings are normally available. In some of the villages accommodation is scarce and in summer particularly it eases the mind during the day to know that a bed for the night is assured. Yet it is unwise to book too far ahead in advance: bad weather may prohibit progress as planned and play havoc with a pre-arranged programme, and it is better to book ahead after breakfast, each morning, by telephone, only if the weather is favourable. Youth hostellers are well served, most of the way, but on three nights must seek other accommodation or sleep under the stars.

Given reasonable weather, the walk can be done in two weeks, not rushing it nor trailing behind schedule. A very strong athlete might do it in a week, but this is a walk that ought to be done in comfort and for pleasure or not at all.

Some readers who would like to do the walk may, for a variety of reasons, prefer to tackle the sections at intervals of time and possibly not in sequence, travelling from home on each occasion: this practice has other advantages, notably avoidance of the need to reserve a bed and the selection of fine clear days only, while leaving you free to go to Majorca for your main holiday if your wife keeps on nagging about it. Everybody has a car these days, even me (and, in my case, a good-looking, competent chauffeur to go with it) and most sections of the route are within reach of the urban areas in the northern counties. The route detailed in this book is my own preference, but some walkers may choose to vary it in places, either to make additional detours or to short-cut corners, or even follow their own course over lengthy distances. Such personal initiatives are to be encouraged — if they do not involve trespass. The way you go and the time it takes matter not. The essence of the walk is the crossing of England, from one coast to the other, on foot.

The walk is described from west to east. It is generally better in this country to walk from the west or south so as to have the weather on your back and not in your face. In the case of this particular walk it is perhaps unfortunate that the grandest part of it, through Lakeland, comes so early, but those who do not already know the heather moors of north-east Yorkshire can be assured that they form a fitting climax.

Robin Hood's Bay

THE SECTIONS
OF THE ROUTE

SECTION MAP : *ST. BEES to ENNERDALE BRIDGE* : 14¼ miles

IRISH SEA

Whitehaven

A.5086

Ennerdale Bridge

ST. BEES HEAD

Sandwith

A.595

Cleator Moor

Cleator

DENT

RHB

St. Bees

START

Egremont

Detailed maps and narrative — on pages 1 - 11

St. Bees

Saint Bees (always abbreviated to St. Bees) is an ancient community with deep-rooted ecclesiastical and scholastic foundations. Here was established a nunnery in the 7th century by St. Bega, this being succeeded on the site by a Benedictine Priory in the 12th century. After the dissolution of the monasteries the Priory, then ruinous, was restored and adopted as the present Parish Church under the name of the Priory Church of St. Mary and St. Bega. The original fabric has largely been superseded in the course of later alteration and repair but some interesting features remain, notably the west doorway, erected in 1150: a splendid example of Norman architecture.

The Grammar School, known nationally, was founded in 1583 by the then Archbishop of Canterbury under a charter granted by Queen Elizabeth I. It is set around an elegant quadrangle opposite the Church, both buildings being constructed of the red sandstone so much in evidence locally.

The village straggles the sheltered valley of Pow Beck through which runs the main railway serving the towns of west Cumberland. The coast, half a mile away, is the modern attraction with its extensive sands beyond a massive concrete seawall, built in 1959-61 to prevent erosion, and wide areas of colourful boulders, some of them fallen from the cliffs, others deposited here from the inland mountains by the retreating glaciers long ago.

— *The west doorway, Priory Church.*

Section map amended 1994

*The Priory Church,
St. Bees*

St. Bees Head

North of the foreshore at St. Bees rises the lofty bulwark of St. Bees Head, four miles of towering and precipitous cliffs of red sandstone veined with white, the haunt and nesting place of countless seabirds and a rich habitat of flowers, the whole making a gay and colourful scene, especially in springtime.

There are two main headlands, North Head and South Head, at an average height of 300 feet, divided near Fleswick Bay by a rocky gully. A lighthouse, a coastguard station and a series of observation huts testify to the shipping hazards in these waters.

It is along the top of the cliffs, in the company of a continuous wire fence, that this long journey to Robin Hood's Bay begins.

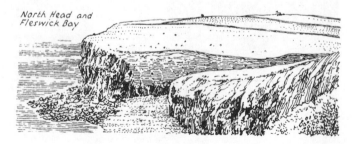

*North Head and
Fleswick Bay*

The walk starts from the sea wall. Rather disconcertingly (because we are supposed to be heading due EAST across England to the Yorkshire coast) it aims WEST, following the cliff, soon changing course to the north. A continuous fence along the rim of the cliff, with stiles, is a sure guide — there is no possibility of getting lost but there is a risk of accident on the seaward side of the fence: assurance of ultimately arriving at Robin Hoods Bay is much greater if the landward side is preferred. The walk is straightforward and easy, with superb views in retrospect and exciting peeps down to the sea 300 feet below.

There are a few other features of interest:
* Pattering Holes, enclosed by a fence, is a curious fissure with conflicting legends about its origin.
* The cliff-edge ruin is a former coastguard station.
* Fallen telegraph poles littering the fields are relics of a disused communication system with the lighthouse. The Parish Council ought to get these removed from the scene.
* The observation hut, one of several along this coast, is adorned with a notice: 'CROWN PROPERTY. NOTHING VALUABLE INSIDE. PLEASE DO NOT DAMAGE.'
* A prominent column 120 yards inland from the observation hut holds promise of a runic cross but a visit reveals the truth — it is merely a scratching post for sheep.

The hinterland of the cliffs is patterned with old sandstone walls, some overgrown and in decay, others reinforced with wire fences. They are omitted from this map except where they impinge on the path.

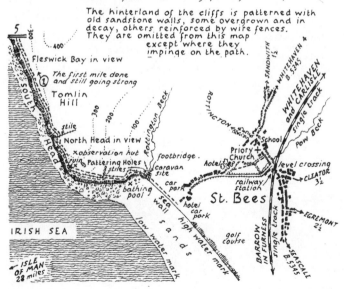

4

North Head

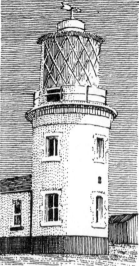

St. Bees Lighthouse

The lighthouse occupies an exposed site 150 yards inland from the cliffs of the North Head at an altitude of 310 feet. It is a white-painted structure with keepers' cottages and outbuildings adjoining. The first lighthouse here was established in 1717 but was destroyed by fire and replaced in 1822. The present structure dates from 1866. Its light is visible at sea for 25 miles.

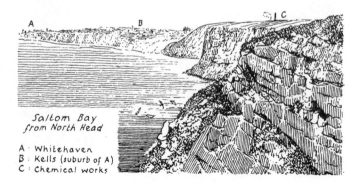

Saltom Bay
from North Head

A : Whitehaven
B : Kells (suburb of A)
C : Chemical works

SOUTH HEAD to SANDWITH

Fleswick Bay, the most beautiful part of the coast, will not be passed unnoticed. A great gash in the cliffs requires a steep descent to sea level (on a wellworn path) and a steep ascent out (including an easy 18' rock climb). By detouring inland a short way this loss and recovery of height could be avoided, but DO go down to the beach to see the splendid rock scenery, caves, pebbles, and hanging gardens of flowers.
Then proceed by the fence to the lighthouse. From here a private road (walkers have a right of way) goes to Sandwith but instead of using it continue along the cliff-top, which soon turns east to disclose a fine view of Saltom Bay and Whitehaven, with Criffell and the hills of Galloway beyond across the Solway Firth. Keep on by the fence, the path here being mostly on the seaward side, to the great crater of a disused quarry, where pass round two cottages into a lane floored with red sandstone and sunken between green banks to join the private road going down to Sandwith, a pleasant village with more inns than churches. Turn left.

Saltom Bay

Birkhams
Quarry (disused)
cottages

IRISH SEA

crops
stile (keep
close
to fence)
wall
4
lane

private road
to lighthouse
but a public
footpath
300

detached
buttress
stiles
300

3
stiles
300

x air shaft
reservoir
Sandwith
6

stiles
x hut
Coastguard
Station
stile
Tarnflat
Hall

Anhydrite mines for the
chemical works nearby
penetrate far under
St. Bees Head.

ST. BEES 12

St. Bees Lighthouse

'Sandwith' is pronounced 'Sanith'
'Fleswick' is pronounced 'Flezzick'

ROTTINGTON

gateway
or stile

St.
Bees
Head

2
stile

rockclimb
to
hut
gate
stile
stile
detour

caves

The 'business part' of the lighthouse may be
inspected by arrangement with the keeper,
but remember time is short.

It is galling to find on arrival at Sandwith
after walking five miles that St. Bees is less
than two miles distance and that you are
actually further west of Robin Hood's Bay
than at the start. Never mind. St. Bees
Head was well worth the detour and now
at Sandwith you can face east and march
towards it with resolution.
Incidentally, Sandwith would be a good
first night's objective in the event of an
afternoon start from St. Bees. Ring 'The
Lowther Arms' before setting forth.

Fleswick
Bay

stile

3

The Whitehaven Chemical Works
(Marchon Products and Solway Chemicals)

Even more conspicuous than the lighthouse is the vast array of chimneys, towers and sheds at the chemical plants on the Whitehaven side of St. Bees Head. The development of these works, and their rapid expansion has been a remarkable and romantic success story, bringing prosperity to a district that suffered severe depression between the wars with the decline in production of coal and iron, on which its economy had been based. It was due to the iniative and foresight of mid European industrialists, refugees from Hitler's regime, that this modern enterprise was introduced around 1940.   A local mineral, anhydrite, long thought of little commercial value, forms the basis of its products of sulphuric acid and cement, and also produced here are detergent chemicals and phosphates.

These works have added nothing of amenity or scenic values to the landscape and inevitably have further devastated a sad area already badly scarred by the rubbish dumps of abandoned iron ore mines and smelting works, spoil heaps and derelict railways.   But man must live, somehow— and here he has, as compensation for his man-despoiled environment, a background of undefiled hills, the beautiful western fells of Lakeland, only ten miles distant — and the complete antithesis of urban ugliness.

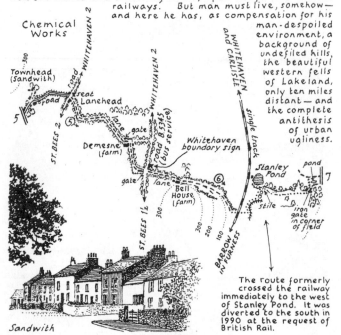

Chemical Works

Townhead (Sandwith)

Great Lanehead

Demesne (farm)

Whitehaven boundary sign

Bell House (farm)

Stanley Pond

pond

iron gate in corner of field

stile

Sandwith

The route formerly crossed the railway immediately to the west of Stanley Pond. It was diverted to the south in 1990 at the request of British Rail.

Leaving Sandwith the road rises in a curve to Lanehead, the huge chemical works being nearby on the left; better to look at is the view ahead to the green hill of Dent and the lofty mountains beyond. At Lanehead continue on the lane facing to the farm of Demesne, where pass through the yard, turning right to reach the Whitehaven-St.Bees road. Cross it and go along the lane opposite, passing Bell House on the right. Ignore a track branching off to the left, but when the track divides in the next field take the left fork, which leads to a gate. Don't go through it, but continue straight on, following the right-hand side of a hedge to the main-line railway. Pass under the railway, and cut across the field ahead to a sinuous fence (the former course of Pow Beck). Follow this to the left, and continue along the side of a hedge to the field corner, where there is a stile on the right.

Get over it and proceed to the top of the next pasture where a wicket gate in the left corner admits to a gated cart-track going uphill under a railway bridge (last view here of St. Bees, still only two miles away!!) to reach the busy main road A595. Scurry across it to the road opposite signposted 'Moor Row' and follow this (Scalegill Road) to the village centre, where turn to the right on the Egremont road. Over the first rise look out for a stile on the left, in the hedge — this stile is the key to a field-path that goes across the railway and leads pleasantly into Church Street, Cleator.

*Road walking may be avoided by joining the Whitehaven to Ennerdale Cycle Path (a disused railway) to the west of the A595 and leaving it at Dalzell Street, or continuing along the Egremont extension to the level crossing.

At Cleator there is an opportunity to interrupt the walk in case of emergency (including weary limbs) by taking a bus to Egremont nearby for an overnight stay: several hotels and bed and breakfast places — and a castle ruin. Chip shops, too.

Map amended 1994.

Cleator

Cleator ("the outlying pasture among the rocks") is an old village that expanded with the boom in iron-ore mining last century and in so doing sacrificed its charm and character. Some architectural pretensions are evident in its places of worship and a few older houses but completely absent in the long terraces of small cottages built to a common pattern to provide for the rapid influx of miners. Brave attempts are being made to improve these dwellings but it needs more than can come out of a tin of paint to make them attractive visually. The mines have closed; the homes of their workers remain amongst the scars as cheerless monuments to a brief prosperity that withered and died. Other mining communities nearby are similarly afflicted. Cleator Moor, a mile to the north, is a newer and larger village directly attributable to industrial development.

Travellers through these places in search of four-star rest and refreshment can abandon hope: they make no claim to be holiday resorts or tourist centres. The primary concern of the inhabitants is to earn a living for themselves, not to cater for the leisure of others.

St. Leonards Church

The Parish Church of Cleator, dedicated to St. Leonard, appears at first glance to be a modern building of red sandstone, but in fact the structure contains masonry dating from the 12th century, when an earlier church stood on this site, and remains of even more ancient walls found here suggest the possibility of a pre-Norman church.

The view from Dent

The green hill of Dent, once partly a deer park, is an excellent viewpoint, with a panorama far wider than its modest elevation would suggest. The whole of the Cumberland coastal plain from Black Combe to the Solway is seen without interruption, dotted with towns and villages as on a map. The Isle of Man is fully in view, looking surprisingly near, and if visibility is really good it might be possible to settle an old argument — whether the Irish mountains can be seen from Dent. But on the ascent from the west it is the sudden revelation of the Lakeland fells that rivets the attention, the prospect being unexpectedly good and ranging clockwise from the Loweswater Fells (overtopped by Skiddaw and Grasmoor) to the High Stile and Pillar groups enclosing Ennerdale, and then, best of all, a fine silhouette of Scafell Pike and Scafell. The only lake in view is Ennerdale Water, not seen to full extent.

The summit
of Dent

SCAFELL

SCAFELL PIKE

Church Street leads into the main thoroughfare of Cleator, a busy road with a bus service. Turn left along it and, without wasting time looking for something to eat, in 60 yards go down a side-street on the right ('Kiln Brow') turning right at the bottom of the hill to Blackhow Bridge on the River Ehen (on its way from Ennerdale Water). A lane now ascends gently to the farm of Black How on a quiet byroad. Here an iron gate on the roadside opposite the farmhouse gives access to a cart-track climbing the fell, and oh boy does it feel good to be in open hill country with the industrial belt left behind! The cart-track peters out but it is a simple and straightforward climb alongside a crumbled wall reinforced by a wire fence to the cairn on the summit of Dent. After a good look round, continue in the same direction, crossing a lateral fence to the east ridge of Dent.

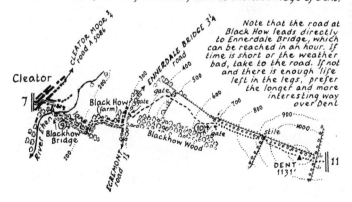

Note that the road at Black How leads directly to Ennerdale Bridge, which can be reached in an hour. If time is short or the weather bad, take to the road. If not and there is enough 'life left in the legs, prefer the longer and more interesting way over Dent

Cleator
7

CLEATOR MOOR ¾
road A 5086

ENNERDALE BRIDGE ¾
road

Black How
(farm)

gate

River Ehen

Blackhow
Bridge

EGREMONT
road 1½

9

200

300

400

500

gate

Blackhow Wood

600

700

gate

800

900

1000

stile

10

DENT
1131'

11

Raven Crag

Nannycatch

Who outside West Cumberland ever heard of Nannycatch? Yet it is within the boundary of the Lake District National Park, and a charming place — a shyly-hidden ravine continuing the much afforested valley of Uldale to the north.

A lovely beckside path runs along this Arcadia-in-miniature beneath the cliffs of Raven Crag.

Kinniside Stone Circle

According to latest information, the Kinniside Stone Circle is a bogus one, which accounts for its omission from Ordnance maps. The story (recounted in earlier books by the author and taken from a source believed to be reputable) that the circle was restored some 50 years ago after the stones had been removed by local farmers, is now regarded as a fib, the true fact being that the stones were arranged on the site merely as an example of a prehistoric circle, by a local archaeologist

Ennerdale Bridge

Ennerdale Bridge is a convenient halting place at the end of the first day. It is a quiet hamlet, known to West Cumbrians but not to the general Lakes tourist — hence there is not much choice of accommodation. The Fox and Hounds is a comfortable inn in the old tradition; a few nearby cottages and farms take visitors. Note well that the Anglers' Hotel on the shores of Ennerdale Water has been demolished (but may be rebuilt).

DENT to ENNERDALE BRIDGE

As Ennerdale Bridge is approached, an exciting array of impressive mountains comes into view to the east, encircling the long deep valley of Ennerdale.
Now we really are on the threshold of Lakeland.....

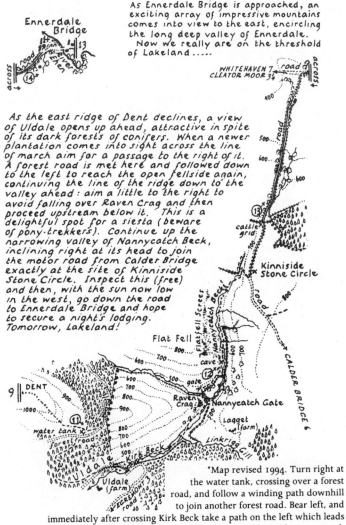

Ennerdale Bridge

WHITEHAVEN 7
CLEATOR MOOR 3¾

As the east ridge of Dent declines, a view of Uldale opens up ahead, attractive in spite of its dark forests of conifers. When a newer plantation comes into sight across the line of march aim for a passage to the right of it. A forest road is met here and followed down to the left to reach the open fellside again, continuing the line of the ridge down to the valley ahead: aim a little to the right to avoid falling over Raven Crag and then proceed upstream below it. This is a delightful spot for a siesta (beware of pony-trekkers). Continue up the narrowing valley of Nannycatch Beck, inclining right at its head to join the motor road from Calder Bridge exactly at the site of Kinniside Stone Circle. Inspect this (free) and then, with the sun now low in the west, go down the road to Ennerdale Bridge and hope to secure a night's lodging. Tomorrow, Lakeland!

Kinniside Stone Circle

Flat Fell

Raven Crag — Nannycatch Gate

Lagget (farm)

DENT

water tank

Uldale (farm)

*Map revised 1994. Turn right at the water tank, crossing over a forest road, and follow a winding path downhill to join another forest road. Bear left, and immediately after crossing Kirk Beck take a path on the left which leads to Nannycatch Gate. The following section of path alongside Nannycatch Beck is not, in fact, a public right of way but the landowners, the National Trust, have generously allowed the route to continue.

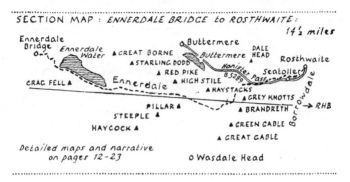

Ennerdale Bridge
Ennerdale Water
▲ GREAT BORNE
▲ STARLING DODD
CRAG FELL ▲
Ennerdale
▲ RED PIKE
▲ HIGH STILE
o Buttermere
Buttermere
DALE HEAD
Honister Pass
B5289
Rosthwaite
Seatoller
▲ HAYSTACKS
▲ GREY KNOTTS
▲ BRANDRETH
▲ GREEN GABLE
▲ GREAT GABLE
PILLAR ▲
STEEPLE ▲
HAYCOCK ▲
→ RHB
Borrowdale

Detailed maps and narrative
on pages 12-23

o Wasdale Head

Ennerdale Water

Ennerdale Water, most westerly of the lakes, is remote from the usual haunts of Lakeland's visitors, yet it lies in a pleasantly rural setting at the outlet of a valley deeply inurned between lofty mountain ranges of which the view across the water is splendid, and in evening sunlight supremely beautiful. The lake, renowned as a fishery for brown trout and char, unobtrusively supplies water to the South Cumberland Water Board. A plan is afoot to raise the level of the lake by a few feet, and in anticipation of this the Anglers' Hotel, which occupied a site at the water's edge (you could fish from its window) has been demolished — prematurely, as events have proved, because nothing else has been done, at the time of writing, to implement the Board's new powers. When the water level is raised a charming pedestrian causeway along the north shore to Bowness Point will be sacrificed, but the rougher path along the south shore is unlikely to be affected.

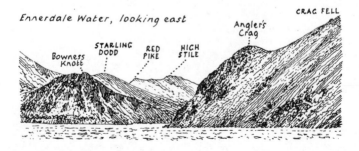

Ennerdale Water, looking east

CRAG FELL
Angler's Crag
BOWNESS KNOTT
STARLING DODD
RED PIKE
HIGH STILE

ENNERDALE BRIDGE to ANGLER'S CRAG

Pillar, from Ennerdale Water

Youth Hostellers have the advantage, on the section to Borrowdale, of three ports of call, but for nonmembers there is no hope of accommodation or refreshment until Seatoller is reached. The walking, however, is easy, with no difficulties of route-finding even in bad weather.

Leave Ennerdale Bridge by the Croasdale road, turning right in half a mile on a side-road to a bridge over the River Ehen. Go round the pumping-house to the lakeside, which then follow to the right, crossing a stile, to the promontory of Angler's Crag. Keep an eye on the pinnacles high above the path.

Map amended 1998.

The steep cliffs of Angler's Crag relent a little just above water level and form a small grassy headland with low rocks. Old maps show this as Robin Hood's Chair, and although the name has gone out of use it seems appropriate to revive it because of its affinity with our ultimate objective: his Bay.

Robin Hood's Chair

The rough ground by the lake at the foot of Angler's Crag was once considered impracticable for pedestrians, but in recent years booted walkers have smoothed the passage and created a track that has a little simple scrambling but no difficulties. Then follows a straightforward walk along the lakeside, wet in places, to the head of the lake, where a green path along the side of a wall is taken, crossing a gap to its north side.

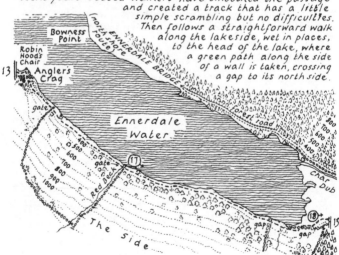

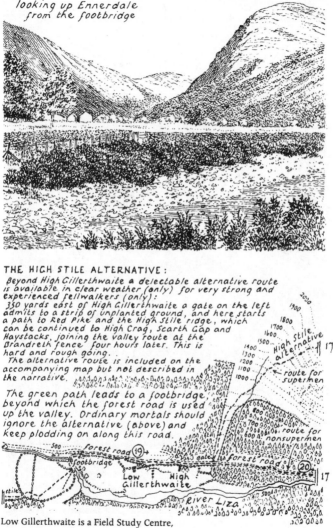

looking up Ennerdale
from the footbridge

THE HIGH STILE ALTERNATIVE:

Beyond High Gillerthwaite a delectable alternative route
is available in clear weather (only) for very strong and
experienced fellwalkers (only):
350 yards east of High Gillerthwaite a gate on the left
admits to a strip of unplanted ground, and here starts
a path to Red Pike and the High Stile ridge, which
can be continued to High Crag, Scarth Gap and
Haystacks, joining the valley route at the
Brandreth fence four hours later. This is
hard and rough going.
The alternative route is included on the
accompanying map but not described in
the narrative.

The green path leads to a footbridge
beyond which the forest road is used
up the valley. Ordinary mortals should
ignore the alternative (above) and
keep plodding on along this road.

Low Gillerthwaite is a Field Study Centre,
privately run; Gillerthwaite is a Youth Hostel, and
High Gillerthwaite Farm has a bunkhouse.

Ennerdale Forest

Where there are now forest roads in Ennerdale there was once a solitary shepherd's track; where there are now plantations of conifers there used to be fellsides open to the sky, singing birds and grazing sheep: it was Herdwick country, Cumberland at its best. Those of us old enough to remember the valley as it was are saddened by the transformation. Lovers of trees paradoxically will not like the hundreds of thousands that make up Ennerdale Forest: deformed, crowded in a battery, denied light and air and natural growth. Trees ought to be objects of admiration, not pity. Trees have life, but thank goodness they have no feelings, else here would be cruelty on a mammoth scale.

Pillar Rock
and the
River Liza

Forestry bridge over the River Liza

The River Liza

The power of a mountain torrent in flood is well exemplified by the River Liza, in dry seasons a wide channel of boulders scoured from the rocky fastnesses at the head of Ennerdale and then rounded and bleached by sun and water, but hidden below a tumultuous cataract in time of spate. The Liza rises near Windy Gap on Great Gable but loses its name in the depths of Ennerdale Water, the outflow being the Ehen

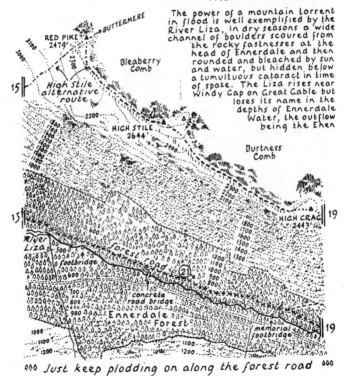

ᗺᗺᗺ *Just keep plodding on along the forest road* ᗺᗺᗺ

looking back to Pillar and Ennerdale from Loft Beck

ENNERDALE FOREST to LOFT BECK

formerly a
shepherd's
hut......

Black Sail Youth Hostel

Black Sail Hut is the loneliest and most romantic of Youth
Hostels, situated in a magnificent surround of mountainous
country. Great Gable dominates the head of the valley with
Green Gable and Kirk Fell in support; looking back, Pillar is
seen soaring above the forest, and High Crag and Haystacks
form an impressive wall to the north. Why go to Switzerland?

The Ennerdale Glacier

The glacier tore away from its moorings on
Great Gable at the end of the Ice Age and
shuffled down to the sea leaving evidence
of its slow journey along the valley. The
forest hides many traces but plain to see
at the open dalehead are stranded
boulders, ice-scratched and polished
rocks and a wide area of drumlins,
the latter, looking like giant
anthills, being clearly in
retrospective view on
the climb up Loft Beck.

All things
come to an end.
Emergence from
the forest is like
coming out of a dark room
into sunlight. Go past the hut
but instead of turning down to the
river contour the slope for half a
mile to Loft Beck, which ascend
steeply by a path on the far bank.

above:
The
Buttermere
valley

left:
Honister
Crag

Honister

Honister is well known for its pass, its crag and its slate. The road through the stony defile, once a fearful adventure for waggonettes but now a smooth way for cars, is, on the Buttermere side, a desert of boulders, one of the roughest wildernesses in Lakeland. Impending high above the pass is Honister Crag, a near-vertical precipice honeycombed with quarries where, in defiance of gravity, a beautiful slate is won and taken down to the cutting sheds. The landscape here has been savaged both by nature and man. What a contrast to their joint efforts in nearby Borrowdale!

At the top of Loft Beck take a last look back to Ennerdale and then continue up an easier incline, crossing a broken wire fence (the Brandreth fence) and contouring along a cairned path to join the Great Gable track coming in from the right; the point of junction is a fine viewing station for the Buttermere valley. The path, much trodden, now leads gently down to the ruined Drum House, where turn right along the old tramway, descending steeply to the road at the top of Honister Pass. Turn right along it, for Borrowdale.

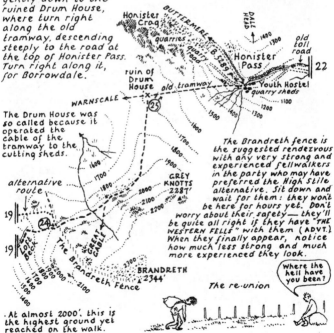

The Drum House was so called because it operated the cable of the tramway to the cutting sheds.

The Brandreth fence is the suggested rendezvous with any very strong and experienced fellwalkers in the party who may have preferred the High Stile alternative. Sit down and wait for them: they won't be here for hours yet. Don't worry about their safety — they'll be quite all right if they have "THE WESTERN FELLS" with them (ADVT.) When they finally appear, notice how much less strong and much more experienced they look.

The re-union

where the hell have you been?

At almost 2000', this is the highest ground yet reached on the walk.

Seatoller

From Honister Pass to Seatoller use the old toll road, which is now quite unsuitable for wheeled traffic but is a good alternative to the new motor road for foot-travellers. At Seatoller (accommodation and café) pass between the houses, turning off at a car park on the left (toilets) to an old walled lane behind: this leads to a path contouring a wooded fellside in lovely surroundings and, accompanied by the River Derwent, reaches Longthwaite Youth Hostel.

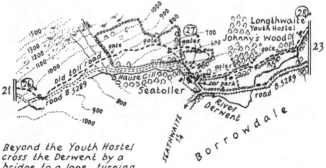

Beyond the Youth Hostel cross the Derwent by a bridge to a lane, turning between the buildings on the left to follow a field-path to the attractive village of Rosthwaite.

Borrowdale

The Lake District is the loveliest part of England, and Borrowdale is the fairest of its valleys. Its appeal lies in the rich tangle of tree and rock — the hanging gardens of birch and rowan, the grey cliffs, that bound its green fields; in its odd configuration, narrowing at mid-valley to the width of road and river but widening at its extremities to form a steep-sided basin for Derwentwater at its foot and a flat strath at its head; in its intriguing side-openings and recesses watered by translucent streams, all beautiful; in its sinuous approach to the highest and finest mountains in the country. Not least of its charms are the clusters of white cottages set amongst its emerald pastures, the centuries-old settlements happily little changed. The picture as a whole is entirely delightful: scenically it is informal to the point of untidyness, yet all things blend in perfect harmony. Man and Nature, working together, have made a good job of Borrowdale.

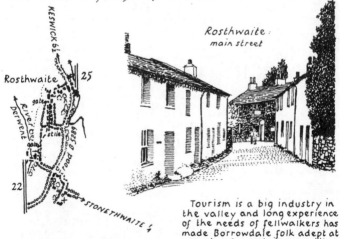

Rosthwaite: main street

Tourism is a big industry in the valley and long experience of the needs of fellwalkers has made Borrowdale folk adept at catering for outsize appetites and tired bodies.

Accommodation is provided in every hamlet and at most farmhouses, and in season is in heavy demand; in addition there are camping and caravan sites and two youth hostels. A walker in search of rest and refreshment for the night is advised to start his enquiries at Rosthwaite, the 'capital' of Borrowdale, which has hotel, guest house, hostel and cottage accommodation. And a very good shop.

SECTION MAP : *ROSTHWAITE to PATTERDALE* : 17½ miles

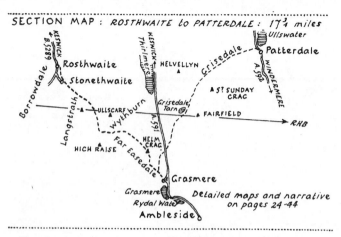

*Detailed maps and narrative
on pages 24-44*

The route onward from Rosthwaite is barred by a line of high fells, the first of a succession of long ridges running north and south across the line of march. These make a direct beeline for the east impracticable, and the most pleasurable way of circumventing the series of obstacles is to take advantage of pedestrian passes through the hills. Such tactics result in considerable deviations both north and south of the "straight and narrow" but the zig-zags recommended will introduce two other places of natural beauty, Grasmere and Patterdale, while at the same time making some longitudinal progress east, albeit erratically. Patterdale is 8 miles due east of Rosthwaite yet the route described covers twice that distance. But the way is lovely and the extra miles will not be regretted. A good walker could reach Patterdale from Rosthwaite comfortably in one day (turning down Wythburn and crossing Dunmail Raise to Grisedale Tarn), but it is more rewarding to proceed slowly in such delectable surroundings and devote two days to the journey with a stop at Grasmere overnight.

The way out of Rosthwaite starts along the valley of Stonethwaite: the only breach in the lofty eastern wall of Borrowdale. It is a walk in heaven.

Stonethwaite

Borrowdale

WATENDLATH

Rosthwaite

23

lane

29

gate

gate

SEATOLLER

B.5289

Stonethwaite Beck

road

gate

Stonethwaite

starry
saxifrage

Eagle Crag

900

DOCK TARN

gate

10

800

400

ruins

600

gate

Galleny
Force

500

1200
1000

800

600

Long Band

500

Langstrath Beck

600

700

gate

21

Greenup Gill

gate

EAGLE
CRAG 1650

1400
1300

1500

1600

1300
1400

1500

1600

32

Lining
Crag

27

Cross the bridge over
Stonethwaite Beck at
Rosthwaite, turning right
along an old lane and then
fields to Stonethwaite
Bridge (which do not cross
except as a detour to look at the
unspoilt and typical hamlet of
Stonethwaite). Continue up the
valley along a gated cart-track
with the beck on the right. In a
short mile there is a junction of
valleys, Langstrath coming down
on the right to a charming meeting
of waters. Do not cross the footbridge
but keep to the good track climbing
steadily alongside Greenup Gill.
Look back at Borrowdale before
the curve of the valley hides it
from sight: a beautiful picture.
The impressive Eagle Crag
loses its fierce aspect
as it is gradually
overtopped. Ahead,
Lining Crag towers
over a prairie of
drumlins. Ascend
a steep stony gully
to the left of it (note
the starry saxifrage)
and detour to its top,
a fine viewpoint, for
a well-earned rest.

route

Lining Crag

The Wythburn trap

Greenup Edge is a pass between Borrowdale and Grasmere, but do not assume that, once over the summit, the ground in front must immediately descend to Grasmere. Beyond the pass for a full half-mile the descending slopes are those of another valley, Wythburn, into which flow the many streams crossed by the path, and it is a common error, especially in mist, to follow the streams down in the belief that they will lead to Grasmere. From Greenup Edge there is a glimpse of Grasmere in clear weather and this sets the true direction.

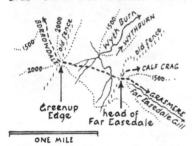

ONE MILE

The path, fairly distinct, skirts the headwaters of the Wythburn basin and after an initial descent levels out before slightly rising to another pass, at 1600', which, like Greenup, is crossed by the remains of a wire fence (including an iron stile incongruously standing in isolation).

This is the true head of Far Easedale, which goes down unerringly, with a good path, to Grasmere.

Let's do a ridge walk

The best form of walking is fell walking and the best part of fell walking is ridge walking and the best part of ridge walking is the traverse of high connecting skylines between neighbouring summits.

So far in this book the route has preferred lower ground, valleys and passes, in the interests of faster progress, but at the head of Far Easedale there is the opportunity of a simple crossing to a miniature ridge of three summits in direct line for Grasmere, offering a more attractive way thereto than the usual route down the valley. This ridge walk adds a mile to the journey, requires an extra effort and takes an hour longer—a small price to pay for the advantages of a delectable track, acquaintance with interesting rock formations, and beautiful views.

So let's do it.

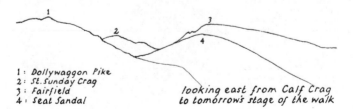

1 : Dollywaggon Pike
2 : St. Sunday Crag
3 : Fairfield
4 : Seat Sandal

looking east from Calf Crag
to tomorrow's stage of the walk

The summit rocks,
Calf Crag

Above Lining Crag the slope eases to Greenup Edge, **the path**
being less distinct over peaty ground : follow the cairns (which
are too numerous), keeping well to the right. The summit of the
pass is marked by an iron stanchion, a relic of a former fence.
The mountain panorama here, especially in retrospect, is grand.
The path continues clearly down the other side, on rough ground
to a lower pass at the head of Far Easedale : on this section do
not be deflected into the valley on the left (Wythburn).
   At the head of Far Easedale there is a choice of routes:
   1 : If the weather is fine and time is not pressing, turn left by
the old fence and follow a thin undulating track over Calf Crag
and beyond down its declining east ridge to Gibson Knott.
   2 : If the weather is poor, or time is short, or you've had enough
climbing for today, or you want to see bog asphodel (a poor excuse)
descend into Far Easedale on a path that soon becomes distinct,
                leading direct, without navigational problems,
                                   to Grasmere in 3½ miles.

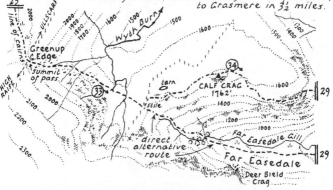

Helm Crag

from Gibson Knott

better known as 'The Lion and the Lamb'

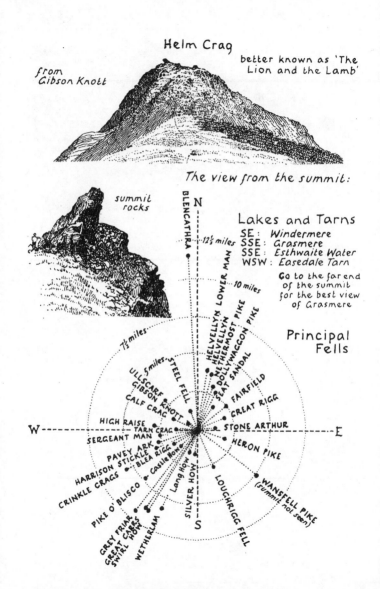

The view from the summit:

summit rocks

Lakes and Tarns

SE: *Windermere*
SSE: *Grasmere*
SSE: *Esthwaite Water*
WSW: *Easedale Tarn*

Go to the far end of the summit for the best view of Grasmere

Principal Fells

N

BLENCATHRA

12½ miles

HELVELLYN LOWER MAN

10 miles

HELVELLYN
NETHERMOST PIKE
SEAT SANDAL
DOLLYWAGGON PIKE

FAIRFIELD

7½ miles

GREAT RIGG

STEEL FELL
ULLSCARF
5 miles
GIBSON KNOTT
CALF CRAG

STONE ARTHUR

W

HIGH RAISE
TARN CRAG
SERGEANT MAN

HERON PIKE

E

PAVEY ARK
HARRISON STICKLE
BLEA RIGG
CRINKLE CRAGS
Castle How
Lang How
PIKE O' BLISCO
SILVER HOW
LOUGHRIGG FELL
WANSFELL PIKE
(summit not seen)

GREY FRIAR
GREAT CARRS
SWIRL HOW
WETHERLAM

S

Grasmere

Grasmere is a lovely village in a setting endowed with sylvan grace and dignity, beloved of artists and poets, and, because of associations with Wordsworth, is known internationally and has become a place of pilgrimage. It is an excellent overnight halting stage, with much to see and a wide choice of accommodation for both primitive and sophisticated walkers.

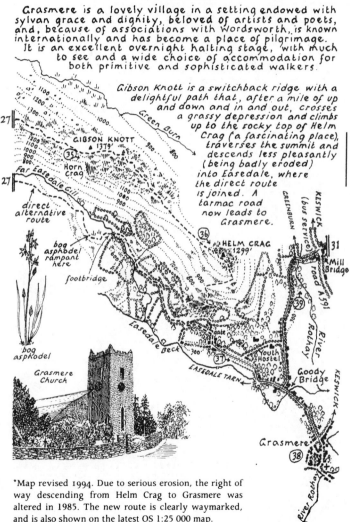

Gibson Knott is a switchback ridge with a delightful path that, after a mile of up and down and in and out, crosses a grassy depression and climbs up to the rocky top of Helm Crag (a fascinating place), traverses the summit and descends less pleasantly (being badly eroded) into Easedale, where the direct route is joined. A tarmac road now leads to Grasmere.

GIBSON KNOTT △ 1379'

Horn Crag

Green Burn

Far Easedale Gill

direct alternative route

bog asphodel rampant here

footbridge

bog asphodel

GREENBURN

KESWICK (bus service)

HELM CRAG △ 1299'

road A591

31 Mill Bridge

River Rothay

Easedale Beck

gate

Grasmere Church

Easedale Tarn

Youth Hostel

Goody Bridge

KESWICK

Grasmere

River Rothay

*Map revised 1994. Due to serious erosion, the right of way descending from Helm Crag to Grasmere was altered in 1985. The new route is clearly waymarked, and is also shown on the latest OS 1:25 000 map.

Grisedale Pass

The pedestrian route from Grasmere to Patterdale, a splendid walk, lies over the wellknown Grisedale Pass (more correctly but less often named Grisedale Hause), a high corridor reaching 1929 feet between very imposing mountains, typically Lakeland in its atmosphere and character: romantically beautiful at start and finish but sombre and austere in the lofty middle section. A notable feature is Grisedale Tarn at 1768 feet, a large sheet of water in a bowl formed by bare hills; and a most striking and impressive picture is displayed soon afterwards by the wild and craggy eastern coves of the Helvellyn range overlooking the fine valley of Grisedale, the descent into which is a remarkable transition from savage desolation to pastoral loveliness. The path, also used in the ascent of Helvellyn, is welltrodden and distinct throughout.

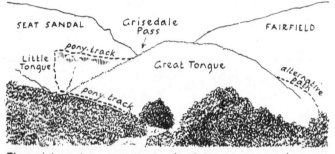

SEAT SANDAL   Grisedale Pass   FAIRFIELD

Little Tongue   pony-track   Great Tongue   alternative path

pony-track

The point of departure from the Grasmere valley is a mile north of the village at Mill Bridge on the main road (A.591) to Keswick and is best reached by a quiet byroad turning off the Easedale road at Goody Bridge: this has a fine view up Tongue Gill to Grisedale Pass. At Mill Bridge go up a lane usually signposted 'To Helvellyn and Patterdale', climbing by the wooded beck to a confluence of streams at the bottom of Great Tongue. Either side of Great Tongue may be taken: it is usual to bear left on a pony-track and climb Little Tongue (a tedious ascent on grass) for the sake of the retrospective views of Grasmere; at 1600' the track turns to the right above a fringe of rocks and becomes undulating before rising amid stones to the top of Grisedale Pass. (The alternative path east of Great Tongue, starting at a footbridge, is easier; it finally joins the pony-track beyond a series of cascades). The summit of the pass is crossed by an old wall and here there is a view forward of Grisedale Tarn backed by Dollywaggon Pike with a zig-zag scar indicating the Helvellyn path. Descend to the outlet of the tarn and make a decision (see page 34).

GRASMERE to GRISEDALE

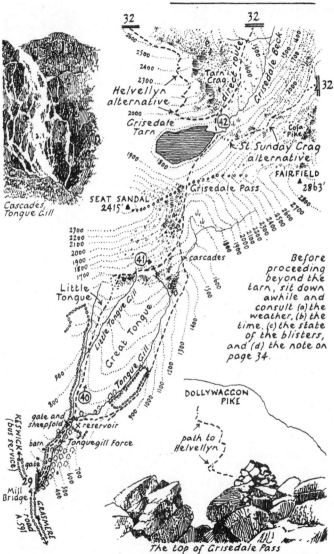

32   32

2600
2500
2400
2300

Helvellyn
alternative

2000

Grisedale
Tarn

1900

1800

32

Tarn
Crag

Grisedale
Beck

1500
1600

1500 1400
1600

1700
1800
1900
2000

direct route

42

Cofa
Pike

32

St. Sunday Crag
alternative

FAIRFIELD
▲ 2863'

Cascades,
Tongue Gill

SEAT SANDAL
2415' ▲

Grisedale Pass

2700
2600
2500
2400
2300
2200
2100
2000
1900

2300
2200
2100
2000
1900
1800
1700

41 →

← cascades

1800
1900
1600

500

Little
Tongue

Little Tongue Gill

Great Tongue

Tongue Gill

40

900

800

KESWICK ←
(bus service)

gate and
sheepfold

× reservoir

barn Tonguegill Force

gate

29

Mill
Bridge

GRASMERE
road
A.591

700

600
500
400

800

700

1000
1100
1200
1300
1400
1500
1600

1300

Before
proceeding
beyond the
tarn, sit down
awhile and
consult (a) the
weather, (b) the
time, (c) the state
of the blisters,
and (d) the note on
page 34.

DOLLYWAGGON
PIKE

path to
Helvellyn

The top of Grisedale Pass

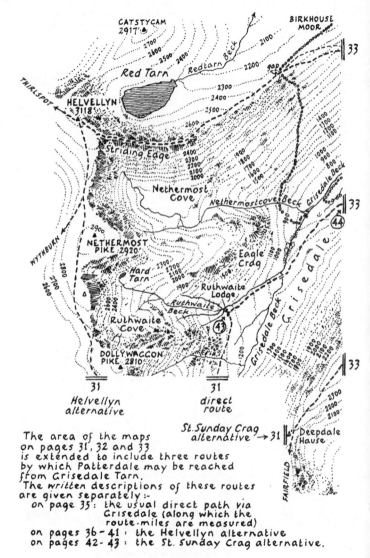

The area of the maps
on pages 31, 32 and 33
is extended to include three routes
by which Patterdale may be reached
from Grisedale Tarn.
The written descriptions of these routes
are given separately:—

on page 35: the usual direct path via
                Grisedale (along which the
                route-miles are measured)
on pages 36-41: the Helvellyn alternative
on pages 42-43: the St. Sunday Crag alternative.

GRISEDALE to PATTERDALE

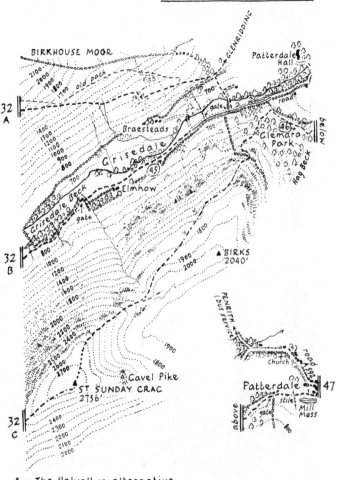

A : The Helvellyn alternative
B : The direct route
C : The St. Sunday Crag alternative

The 'St.' in the name 'St. Sunday Crag' is an abbreviation for 'Saint' (as in St.Bees), not 'Street'.

Let's climb a mountain

The outlet of Grisedale Tarn is a splendid springboard for climbing a mountain on the way to Patterdale (in preference to the direct route, which here commences the long descent into Grisedale), and, if Grasmere was left after breakfast, there should be ample time in hand to do this. The tarn is at 1800', nearly, so that at this point a considerable elevation has already been reached and if the day be fine and settled it seems a pity not to use the height gained to make the ascent of one of the surrounding mountains before taking leave of the Lake District (tomorrow). Lakeland means, to most visitors, not lakes but mountains, and it is fitting that a walk across the district should include a high summit.

Okay then, which one? Well, the two most convenient are HELVELLYN and ST. SUNDAY CRAG, each having a ridge descending to Patterdale. The choice lies between them. The ascent of Helvellyn (3118') would add two miles and 1500' of climbing to the walk and take two hours longer than the direct route. It has two big attractions apart from its lovely name and literary associations — a very extensive view and the exciting traverse of Striding Edge — but it is a tourists' mountain, very much so: in fact, the most often climbed mountain in the country. The paths, worn as wide as roads, are stony and dusty and noisy with pilgrims.

St. Sunday Crag (2756') is, in sharp contrast, a mountain for connoisseurs: lovely to walk upon, unspoiled, quiet and free from crowds and their attendant litter. It has a classic view of Ullswater. Its ascent would add 1000' of climbing and take an extra hour compared with the way down the valley but in distance is no further.

Walkers who have not yet climbed Helvellyn (if any such there be) will probably prefer to do this. Walkers who have are recommended to try St. Sunday Crag. Neither ascent calls for superhuman ability.

If the rain is pouring down, contemplate neither but go down into Grisedale by the usual direct route.

St. Sunday Crag, from the outlet of Grisedale Tarn

looking down Grisedale from Ruthwaite

Grisedale Tarn to Patterdale
— the direct route

The direct path to Patterdale along Grisedale is distinct on the ground and calls for little description to supplement the map but certain interesting features are worth mention. Ford the stream issuing from Grisedale Tarn and follow the path ahead, bearing right. Note an outcrop surmounted by a metal sign 60 yards away on the right — this is the Brothers Parting, the place where Wordsworth said a last farewell to his brother John: his verses are inscribed on the rockface. A mile further, the path reaches Ruthwaite Lodge, built in 1854 by the then owner of Patterdale Hall as a rest-house for passing travellers and now occupied by the University Mountaineering Club, Sheffield. Behind the Lodge are pleasant cascades and old mine levels. The path now descends more sharply by the side of Ruthwaite Beck to a footbridge over Grisedale Beck. In scenery that grows more beautiful every step of the way along the valley, the path continues clearly below the steep slopes of St. Sunday Crag and Birks, becoming a cart-track near the farm at Elmhow and a tarmac road half-a-mile further. Cars parked in a field indicate the point where the Helvellyn path joins, and 350 yards further, beyond a plantation, a gate on the right gives access to a pleasant path through Glemara Park to Patterdale Post Office.

Brothers Parting

Ruthwaite Lodge

Grisedale Tarn to Patterdale
— the Helvellyn alternative

Gird up your loins, ford the stream issuing from the tarn and bear left to the distinct path climbing up the steep slope in front in a series of zigzags. The gradient eases after an eternity of toil and the path forges ahead rounding the summits of Dollywaggon Pike and Nethermost Pike and finally rising to the top of Helvellyn. In spite of its stones and litter and crowds this is a fine high-level traverse, improved by detours to the right to look down in the vast hollows on the eastern side of the range. If the visibility on Helvellyn is good the panorama pictured on pages 38 to 41 can be checked for accuracy, after which, carefully stepping over the recumbent bodies of exhausted tourists, follow the rim of the summit southeast to Gough's monument, there descending the loose and stony declivity to Striding Edge — an unpleasant descent. Getting onto the Edge involves an awkward preliminary scramble up rocks, but thereafter an easy path runs along it slightly below the crest on the Red Tarn side : this is an exhilarating traverse (the best quarter-mile between St. Bees and Robin Hood's Bay) and it should be lingered over, with frequent moves onto the actual rock crest to savour the airiness of the situation and look for Dixon's Monument. Beyond the dark tower at the end of the Edge life becomes ordinary again and the path gently runs along a declining ridge, passes through a gap in a wall, and slants down the flank of Birkhouse Moor to cross a bridge over Grisedale Beck in the valley and so join a tarmac road. Turn left along it and 350 yards further, beyond a plantation, a gate on the right gives access to a pleasant path through Glemara Park to Patterdale Post Office.

The Monuments of Helvellyn —

The Gough Memorial

Erected 1890 on the rim of the summit above the path to Striding Edge.

This small stone tablet 40 yards south of the shelter commemorates the landing here of an aeroplane in 1926 — a memorable event!

The Dixon Memorial 1858

Situated on a platform of rock on Striding Edge overlooking Nethermost Cove and Grisedale.

Striding Edge

The view from Helvellyn

The figures following the names of fells indicate distances in miles

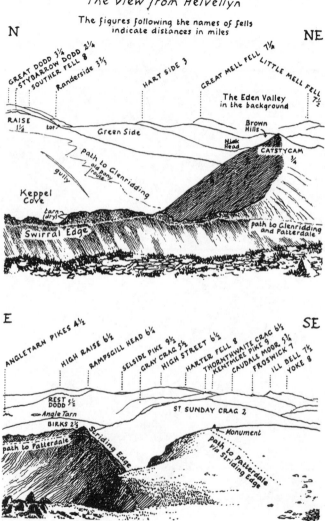

The view from Helvellyn

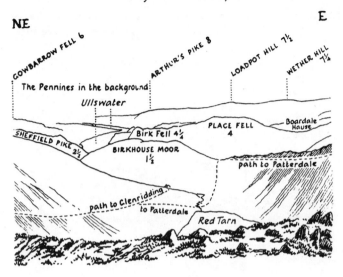

NE   E

GOWBARROW FELL 6

ARTHUR'S PIKE 8

LOADPOT HILL 7½

WETHER HILL 7¼

The Pennines in the background

Ullswater

Boardale Hause

PLACE FELL 4

SHEFFIELD PIKE 2½

Birk Fell 4¼

BIRKHOUSE MOOR 1½

path to Patterdale

path to Glenridding

to Patterdale

Red Tarn

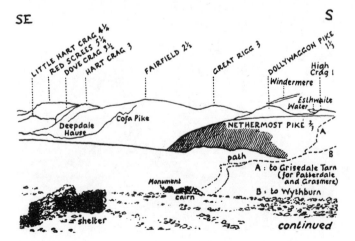

SE   S

LITTLE HART CRAG 4¼
RED SCREES 5¼
DOVE CRAG 3½
HART CRAG 3

FAIRFIELD 2½

GREAT RIGG 3

DOLLYWAGGON PIKE 1½

High Crag 1

Windermere

Esthwaite Water

Deepdale Hause

Cofa Pike

NETHERMOST PIKE ⅔

A

path

B

Monument
cairn

A : to Grisedale Tarn (for Patterdale and Grasmere)

B : to Wythburn

shelter

continued

The view from Helvellyn

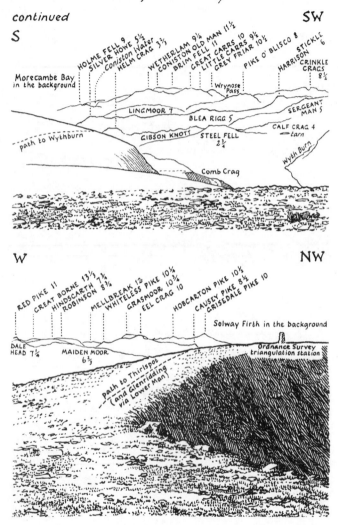

continued

S   SW

HOLME FELL 9 5½
SILVER HOWE 5½
Coniston Water 3⅓
HELM CRAG 3⅓
WETHERLAM 9¼
CONISTON OLD MAN 11½
BRIM FELL 11
GREAT CARRS 10
LITTLE CARRS 9½
GREY FRIAR 10½
PIKE O' BLISCO 8
HARRISON
STICKLE 6
CRINKLE CRAGS 8½

Morecambe Bay
in the background

Wrynose
Pass

LINGMOOR 7

BLEA RIGG 5

SERGEANT
MAN 5

path to Wythburn

GIBSON KNOTT

STEEL FELL
2¼

CALF CRAG 4
← tarn

Wyth Burn

Comb Crag

W   NW

RED PIKE 11
GREAT BORNE 13⅓
HINDSCARTH 7½
ROBINSON 8¾
MELLBREAK 12
WHITELESS PIKE 10½
GRASMOOR 10¾
EEL CRAG 10
HOBCARTON PIKE 10½
CAUSEY PIKE 8½
GRISEDALE PIKE 10

Solway Firth in the background

DALE
HEAD 7½

MAIDEN MOOR
6⅓

Ordnance Survey
triangulation station

path to Thirlspot
(and Glenridding
via Lower Man)

The view from Helvellyn

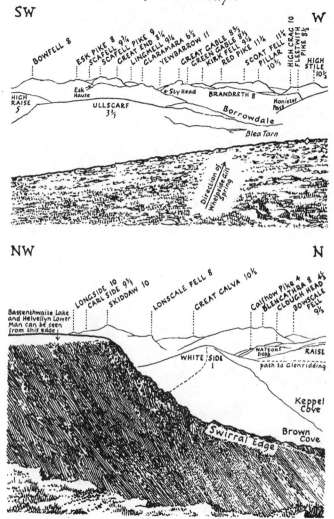

SW · W

BOWFELL 8 · ESK PIKE 8 · SCAFELL 9¾ · SCAFELL PIKE 9 · GREAT END 8½ · LINGMELL 9¼ · GLARAMARA 6½ · YEWBARROW 11 · GREAT GABLE 8½ · GREEN GABLE 8½ · KIRK FELL 9¼ · RED PIKE 11½ · SCOAT FELL 11½ · PILLAR 10¾ · HIGH CRAG 10 · FLEETWITH PIKE 8½ · HIGH STILE 10½

HIGH RAISE 5 · Esk Hause · ULLSCARF 3⅓ · ←Sty Head · BRANDRETH 8 · Honister Pass · Borrowdale

Blea Tarn

Direction of Whelpside Gill Spring

NW · N

Bassenthwaite Lake and Helvellyn Lower Man can be seen from this edge ↓

LONGSIDE 10 · CARL SIDE 9⅔ · SKIDDAW 10 · LONSCALE FELL 8 · GREAT CALVA 10½ · Calfhow Pike · BLENCATHRA 8 · CLOUGH HEAD 4½ · BOWSCALE FELL 9½

WHITE SIDE 1 · WATSONS DODD · RAISE · path to Glenridding

Keppel Cove

Brown Cove

Swirral Edge

Grisedale Tarn to Patterdale
— the St. Sunday Crag alternative

At the outlet of the tarn turn to the right (east) without crossing the stream and skirt a pathless marsh until, after 100 yards, cairns and a thin path slant upwards over rough slopes, making a beeline for Deepdale Hause (the depression between Fairfield and St. Sunday Crag).   When the Hause is almost reached a line of cairns leads up to it (leave the path which contours onwards below the ridge) and a magnificent view of the cliffs of Fairfield above the wild upper reaches of Deepdale suddenly unfolds, matching in impressiveness the crags and coves of the Helvellyn range across Grisedale. In the midst of profound mountain scenery follow the ridge up to St. Sunday Crag on a distinct path. Near the top the path is less clear but the way is cairned. Leave the summit bearing north at first, following a line of cairns, then north-east to an outcropping of rocks (a classic viewpoint), beyond which a rough track descends more steeply to the depression before Birks and slants along its western flank high above Grisedale. The route levels out on a grassy shelf and becomes less clear but cairns lead to a made path descending to a wall (crossed at a hurdle) enclosing Glemara Park, through which the path goes down sharp left then right, among trees, to a wire fence. The Grisedale road is now close on the left and can be gained at a gate, but instead turn right, by a wall, on a delightful path that fords Hag Beck and skirts Mill Moss, rampant with rushes and bogbean, just behind Patterdale Post Office.

Ullswater, from the north-east ridge of St. Sunday Crag

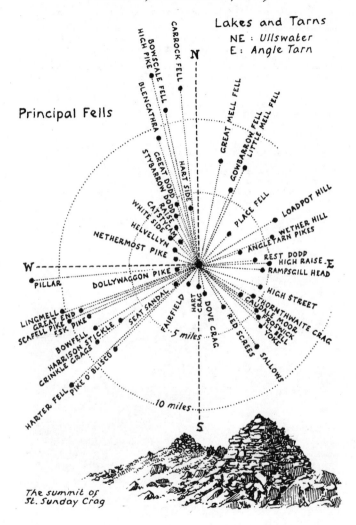

The view from St. Sunday Crag

43

Principal Fells

Lakes and Tarns
NE : Ullswater
E : Angle Tarn

N
E
W
S

CARROCK FELL
HIGH PIKE
BOWSCALE FELL
BLENCATHRA
GREAT MELL FELL
LITTLE MELL FELL
GOWBARROW FELL
GREAT DODD
STYBARROW DODD
HART SIDE
RAISE
CATSTYCAM
WHITE SIDE
HELVELLYN
NETHERMOST PIKE
PLACE FELL
LOADPOT HILL
WETHER HILL
ANGLETARN PIKES
REST DODD
HIGH RAISE
RAMPSGILL HEAD
PILLAR
DOLLYWAGGON PIKE
HIGH STREET
THORNTHWAITE CRAG
CAUDALE MOOR
FROSWICK
ILL BELL
YOKE
SALLOWS
LINGMELL
GREAT END
SCAFELL PIKE
ESK PIKE
BOWFELL
HARRISON STICKLE
CRINKLE CRAGS
SEAT SANDAL
FAIRFIELD
HART CRAG
DOVE CRAG
RED SCREES
HARTER FELL
PIKE O' BLISCO

5 miles

10 miles

The summit of
St. Sunday Crag

Patterdale

Patterdale is a rival to Borrowdale in the magnificence of its surroundings. Dominated on one side by the rugged mountain wall of the Helvellyn range and on the other by the steep flanks of Place Fell, with, between them, that loveliest of lakes, Ullswater, curving gracefully into the far distance; with crags and heathery fells rising from a strath of emerald valley pastures and a wealth of noble trees, the scene is one of informal but exquisite beauty, and the little village is truly Alpine in situation, aspect and character. Although a place of popular resort and a splendid centre for fellwalkers, Patterdale has not as yet suffered the tourist invasions of Borrowdale and remains unspoilt, presenting a picture that has changed very little during the past century.

The provision of accommodation is a main industry here. Many cottages and farmhouses open their doors to visitors, the village has two hotels and there are more a mile away at Glenridding. Goldrill Youth Hostel is an excellent new building in Scandinavian style, opened 1971. In summer all this accommodation is heavily in demand and should be reserved in advance.

Before turning in for the night take a stroll across the valley to the lakeside path below Place Fell for a view of Ullswater that is unsurpassed for loveliness.

The head of Ullswater

46

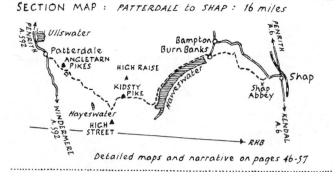

SECTION MAP : *PATTERDALE to SHAP : 16 miles*

Detailed maps and narrative on pages 46-57

The journey from Patterdale to Shap involves a lofty crossing of the High Street massif, the final mountain barrier of Lakeland in the east, and during the course of the walk the scenery changes dramatically, sombre fells giving place to a pastoral limestone landscape. This is farewell to Lakeland, and farewells to Lakeland are always sad. What follows is anti-climax — level walking instead of up and down, trees and fields and villages instead of rough and lonely hills: lovely, yes, but not excitingly beautiful as the crossing of Lakeland has been. Well, it's not too late to abandon the coast to coast idea and stay on in Patterdale. There is nothing ahead as good, admittedly — the big fault of doing this walk in a west to east direction is that the best comes first. Anyway, please yourself. Stay if you want to and I'll carry on alone, and no hard feelings. You'll think of something to tell the folks at home.... Mind, you might find yourself thinking in the next few days about Shap and the limestone plateau beyond, and wondering what Swaledale is really like and whether the North York Moors are as attractive as people say. You *could* have regrets. And (let's be clear about this) you can't expect to get your money back for the book if you prefer not to continue the walk...... Coming with me? Good. I thought you would.

In clear weather the High Street crossing is without difficulties and indeed is a most exhilarating march. If there is rain or mist it is advisable to avoid it (unless the route is remembered from previous visits) and instead use the lakeside path to Howtown followed by a road almost to Pooley Bridge and a path across Moor Divock to Helton; then a quiet road through Bampton to Shap (all clearly shown on the 1" Ordnance map): a long but easy walk (19 miles) that could be shortened by four miles (as can the High Street route) by making Bampton the overnight objective.

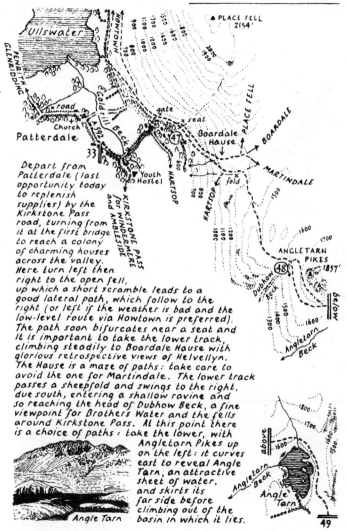

Depart from
Patterdale (last
opportunity today
to replenish
supplies) by the
Kirkstone Pass
road, turning from
it at the first bridge
to reach a colony
of charming houses
across the valley.
Here turn left then
right to the open fell,
up which a short scramble leads to a
good lateral path, which follow to the
right (or left if the weather is bad and the
low-level route via Howtown is preferred).
The path soon bifurcates near a seat and
it is important to take the lower track,
climbing steadily to Boardale Hause with
glorious retrospective views of Helvellyn.
The Hause is a maze of paths: take care to
avoid the one for Martindale. The lower track
passes a sheepfold and swings to the right,
due south, entering a shallow ravine and
so reaching the head of Dubhow Beck, a fine
viewpoint for Brothers Water and the fells
around Kirkstone Pass. At this point there
is a choice of paths: take the lower, with
Angletarn Pikes up
on the left: it curves
east to reveal Angle
Tarn, an attractive
sheet of water,
and skirts its
far side before
climbing out of the
basin in which it lies.

Angle Tarn

The view west from Angle Tarn

ST. SUNDAY CRAG   NETHERMOST PIKE   HELVELLYN   CATSTYCAM

BIRKS

left:
*Kidsty Pike
from Twopenny Crag*

below:
*High Street
from Kidsty Pike*

The 49th mile appears on the 49th page. By a rapid calculation it will be ascertained that we are so far averaging a mile a page.

47

49

Satura Crag

gap

gap

▲ REST DODD
2278'

1800
1700
1600
1500
1400

2200

2100
2000
1900

1400
1700
1800
1900

The valley descending north from Satura Crag is Bannerdale. The valley descending north of The Knott is Rampsgill. They join in Martindale, a deer preserve.

50

gap

The deeply inurned tarn down on this side is Hayeswater (a reservoir). The cluster of buildings lower down its valley is the hamlet of Hartsop.

2000
2100
2200

gap

1900

HARTSOP

THE KNOTT
2423'

stretcher box

RAMPSGILL
HEAD
2581' ▲

HIGH RAISE

2500

2500
2400

KIDSTY PIKE
2560'

51

Twopenny Crag

2000
1900
1800
1700

51

2000
2100
2000
1900
1700

Straits of Riggindale

Riggindale

With Angle Tarn left behind and out of sight the immediate surroundings become dreary. The path continues distinctly, passing over Satura Crag and descending a little to cross wet peaty ground, the only excitement hereabouts being generated by the reflection that fifty miles of the journey have now been accomplished. Already it seems ages since Cleator and Nannycatch! Now follows a tedious climb around the shoulder of The Knott, passing a cairn indicating a track branching off to Hayeswater and Hartsop, and anyone who is regretting having left Patterdale and wishing to return to it for an extended stay (and be damned to the Coast to Coast Walk) may use this pleasant alternative route to do so.

1400

1500

ROMAN ROAD

2400

2500

1700

▲ HIGH STREET
2718'
Ordnance Survey column

Others, more resolute, will toil onwards and reap their reward when, beyond The Knott, they reach a point on the main ridge overlooking a depression (the *Straits of Riggindale*) and find themselves suddenly looking down Riggindale to Haweswater and Mardale Head, with Kidsty Pike and High Street framing the picture. High Street is massively attractive, its Roman road showing clearly, and its summit is easily reached from here but if the hour is already past noon there really isn't time to do it. Instead, take the path branching over Twopenny Crag (named pre-decimalisation) and skirting the rim of Riggindale — very easy walking — to Kidsty Pike: its summit is the best station for taking a last long look at the serrated mountain skyline of Lakeland, the like of which will not be seen again this side of the North Sea. But there will be other years, other visits..... The hills will wait.

The view from Kidsty Pike
(western sector only)

Principal Fells

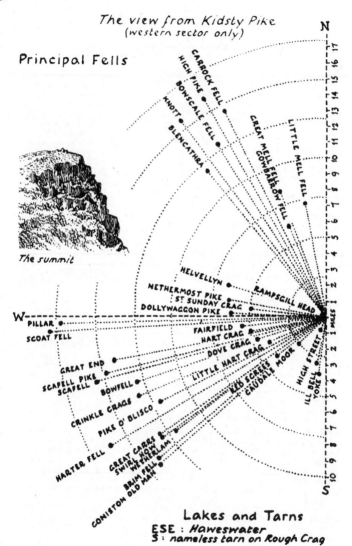

The summit

Lakes and Tarns
ESE : *Haweswater*
S : *nameless tarn on Rough Crag*

The descent from Kidsty Pike is simple. A thin cairned track goes easily down the east ridge but fades before attaining the rocks of Kidsty Howes, whereupon incline left over long grass (hard going) towards Randale Beck. An old drove road may be found, but when this fords the stream near a ruin continue down the west bank to a stone bridge at the foot of the slope. Here are the sad remains of Riggindale Farm, a victim of the transformation of Haweswater into a reservoir.

At the stone bridge the fellside path engineered by Manchester Corporation is reached. Followed to the right it leads to the road-end at Mardale Head in a mile (no accommodation now). Our way is to the left, and although the path is overgrown with bracken in places (especially below Whelter Knotts, where Manchester should send a man with a scythe annually in August) there is no danger of straying from it — it accompanies a wall or fence throughout the full length of the lake (sorry, reservoir) and is nowhere more than 30 yards from it.

The only points of interest are Birks Crag, the top of which is the site of a British fort, and the crossing of Whelter Beck — note the waterfall under the bridge.

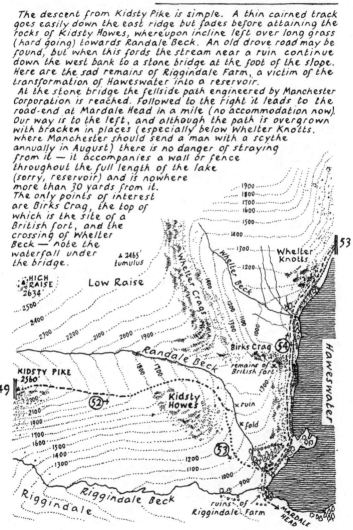

↑ This is what happens when a lake is converted to a reservoir ↓

Mardale

Only those who are getting on in years will remember Mardale as a charming and secluded valley — before its lake was 'promoted' to reservoir, and can bring to mind the natural beaches, where primroses fringed the banks, that are now sterile shores, arid and lifeless, sometimes beneath the water, sometimes not; or the farms and drystone walls that were engulfed and today are revealed as skeletons in times of drought; or the lane that returns to daylight, now recognisable only by tumbled hedgerows, at periods of low water. They mourn its passing, for Mardale then was lovely.

ONE INCH = TWO MILES

Shading indicates the natural Haweswater, the black line the artificial shore of the reservoir.

Church Inn } Mardale Green

HAWESWATER BEFORE AND AFTER

Haweswater from Measand

This section calls for little comment. The way is obvious and straightforward and the path, now improving, is pleasant for both feet and eyes although views of Haweswater along here are obscured by trees. The best natural feature is Measand Forces, a spectacular tangle of rocks and waterfalls, known sufficiently to attract a few visitors on most summer days, the popular approach being from Burn Banks. The path now assumes the width of a cart-track. An item of interest, seen before reaching the Haweswater dam, is the entrance to the reservoir of the tunnelled Heltondale supply, while opposite across the water is glimpsed the outflow of the tunnel from Swindale.

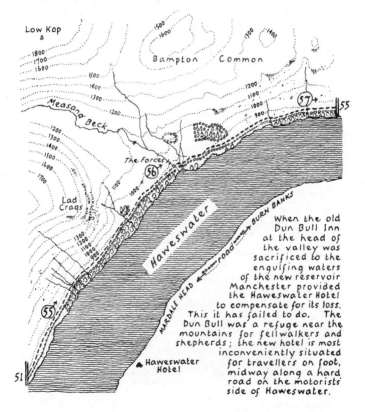

When the old Dun Bull Inn at the head of the valley was sacrificed to the engulfing waters of the new reservoir Manchester provided the Haweswater Hotel to compensate for its loss. This it has failed to do. The Dun Bull was a refuge near the mountains for fellwalkers and shepherds; the new hotel is most inconveniently situated for travellers on foot, midway along a hard road on the motorists' side of Haweswater.

It is a fact that route-finding in cultivated valleys and in low pastures is more prone to error than on desolate mountains. In this section the route follows footpaths (shown on the Ordnance maps) that have obviously fallen into disuse and can no longer be discerned on the ground. Refer to the facing map and following notes as doubts arise. In two places slight variations are shown because of obstructed stiles. These hindrances are a nuisance, coming late in the day, but the scenery is ample compensation.

Burn Banks is reached from a stile in the plantation fence, a road winding down amongst wild raspberries to the neat bungalows of the reservoir employees, set pleasantly among trees. Bear left to the junction of the Bampton and Haweswater roads, turning down the latter. After 120 yards, before reaching a barn, a half-hidden stile in the wall on the left admits to a field, which cross to another stile in the far corner (footpath invisible). so reaching a lane leading to Park Bridge in surroundings that are truly park-like. A cart-track to the left aims for Low Park, but after the second gate go up the field sharp right to High Park, continuing in the same direction, on an invisible footpath, to Rawhead and the Swindale road.

Cross the open common ahead, inclining left to Rosgill Bridge. (Shap can be reached by road from here, saving half an hour). Go through the gate marked 'Good Croft' but, after a second gate, do not follow the road up to the house but keep alongside the wall to a wicket-gate in the corner followed by a stile, then accompanying a fence to a charming packhorse bridge, which, having regard to the obvious non-use of the paths to and from it, is seldom visited. Across it, go up by a hedge to a ruined farm building beyond which is a road. Keep on this road, up the hill, until the wall on the left turns away, then aim half-left to a gate in another wall near trees. Go through (or over) this, noting the ancient dyke here, to another gate on the right, which admits to a large field : go across this, descending to a stile in the far corner with the wooded valley of the River Lowther near ahead. Turn right in the next field to a stile in the wall above Abbey Bridge. Now all is plain sailing. The Abbey is in full view and can be visited. A concrete road climbs the hill beyond the bridge, heading for Shap. Soon be there now...

Packhorse bridge,
Swindale Beck

*Fifty yards after bearing left at Burn Banks, turn right along a woodland path. When you come to the road, take a stile opposite and cross Haweswater Beck by the old bridge alongside Naddle Bridge. Follow the beck downstream to Park Bridge and continue along the cart track ahead.

If exhaustion is imminent there is a fair chance of getting a night's lodging at Bampton, a mile along the road from Burn Banks.

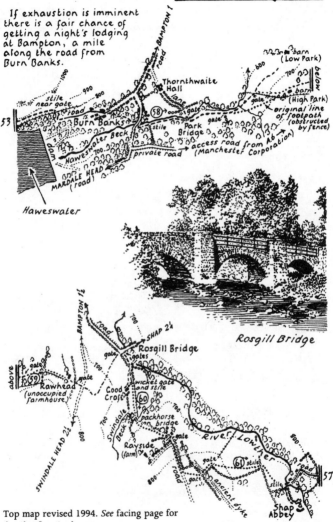

Rosgill Bridge

Top map revised 1994. *See* facing page for details of revised route.

56

Shap Abbey

The builders of England's ancient country abbeys were not only experts in a craft now either extinct or dormant but landscape artists too: they certainly had a good eye for the most-favoured and pleasantest rural locations. Quiet retreats in sequestered valleys, amidst trees and with a river nearby: these were the requisites and it is small wonder that, in such peaceful surroundings, the buildings too had grace and dignity and beauty.

Shap Abbey, built in the 12th and 13th centuries, conforms to this pattern. It stands deep in the wooded valley of the River Lowther, so that it is not seen until the last moments of approach, when the tower reveals its fine proportions. Little else remains above first-floor height and much has been lost, but the arrangement of the various buildings is clear on the ground.

The ruins are in the good care of the Ministry of Public Buildings and Works, who publish a descriptive booklet. A charge is made for admission.

Shap Abbey
from the north

Incidentally (although this has nothing to do with Shap Abbey), that large bird you saw as you came over the mountains from Patterdale might well have been a golden eagle, as you thought. It is now common knowledge that eagles have returned to nest in the Lake District after an absence of more than a century, and successfully reared young, but the location of their eyries is, at the time of writing, a close secret. Our route across the district avoided their nesting places, although in fact they were within sight—at a distance.

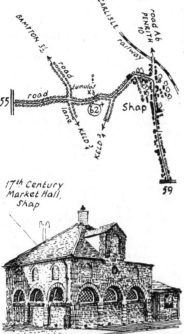

The road, enclosed by walls that provide evidence of our arrival in limestone terrain, leads directly to the north end of Shap village. On the left, over the wall past the first junction, a rounded grassy hump indicates a tumulus. The road joins the once-busy A6. Turn to the right to seek a bed and food.

17th Century Market Hall, Shap

Shap

Shap has been a by-word amongst road travellers since stage-coach days. For many the very name invokes vivid memories of hazardous journeys in snow and storm and mist over the A6, the highest main road in the country, nearly 1400' at its summit in a wilderness of moors. The A6 is a road with a notorious history of accidents but its importance as a main traffic artery to Scotland, however, was greatly diminished at a stroke by the opening on a day in October 1970 of the motorway M6, this taking an easier, lower and less exposed route through the hills. This was a red letter day for some Shap folk, a black letter day for others. The A6 suddenly became quiet. Commerce suffered but, overnight, Shap became a better place to live.

The village straddles the A6 a few miles to the north of its summit: a mile-long village with little breadth, clinging to the road as to a lifeline. It has a few pleasant nooks and corners but is generally unattractive. Its economy is based on the road and railway and especially on the huge granite works and limestone quarries, none of them the source of any beauty or relieving the bleak landscape.

Many hotels and boarding-houses and cafés line the A6, more perhaps than are now required. Shap will live on, but its name will mean nothing to future generations of tourists and lorry-drivers.

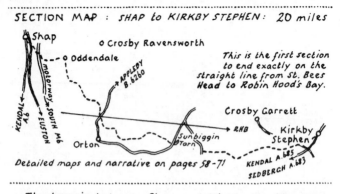

SECTION MAP : *SHAP to KIRKBY STEPHEN*: 20 miles

This is the first section to end exactly on the straight line from St. Bees Head to Robin Hood's Bay.

Detailed maps and narrative on pages 58-71

The terrain between Shap and Kirkby Stephen takes the form of a limestone plateau, elevated at about the 1000' contour, and, as every walker knows, a limestone footing invariably means easy travelling on velvet turf, especially when the rock is outcropping or just below the surface, while its appearance when exposed to weather —crinkled, fissured and often grotesquely sculptured— allied to its glittering whiteness in sunlight, is a delight to the eye always. Mountain limestone is, of course, the great favourite as the basis of rock gardens, and a few areas have been denuded of surface rock stone by exploiters of this demand, but their activities are now, properly, subject to strict planning control. Many of the escarpments and creviced 'pavements' met on the walk are very fine, but the waterworn caves and potholes peculiar to limestone formations are singularly absent in this district.

This section of the walk is also out of the ordinary by reason of its prolific evidences of prehistoric and primitive settlements : hut-villages, stone circles and tumuli are all present in the vicinity, indicating that large communities existed here before the dawn of history, scraping a poor livelihood from land that remains today inhospitable, bare and uncultivated. The ancient settlements near Crosby Ravensworth and Crosby Garrett in particular are of outstanding interest and represent Westmorland's main contribution to archaeological research. Some of these relics of the past will be visited along the route.

The flora of limestone country, too, is a constant joy, the deep crevices harbouring flowers and ferns and mosses in variety; indeed, most limestone outcroppings are complete natural rock gardens furnished with shy and delicate plants, some such as the bird's eye primrose, rare elsewhere, being commonplace locally.

Primula farinosa

A walker on limestone is well favoured.

Section map revised 1994

Paths east of Shap have been disturbed by the motorway, but footbridges have been provided at two points. The village is now most conveniently left by a street directly opposite the Kings Arms Hotel on the A6, leading to a housing estate. Here turn right into a lane bending left to a bridge over the railway, beyond which it runs between walls under an electricity cable. At a fork bear right and cross three fields (the indistinct path is indicated by stiles) to reach a conspicuous footbridge crossing the motorway: an expensive structure for a path so little used. Over the footbridge keep alongside the fence to the right. At a copse of hawthorns a thin track will be found inclining left uphill — note the many granite boulders scattered around — to a gate near a farmhouse (The Nab), through which the road to Hardendale is crossed, the route continuing over a pleasant pasture on the same contour with a limestone scar on the left. When a wall is reached bearing an explosives warning the scene ahead is downright ugly, an active limestone quarry causing widespread devastation. Round the wall corner on the left two stiles admit to the quarry area, where, wonder of wonders, the rights of pedestrians are preserved (the former footpath having been blasted out of existence) by two high flights of wood steps where the access road runs in a deep cutting. Across this road keep on in the same direction, bearing left a little at first, to emerge from the area of devastation to a rough pasture with a good track heading straight for Oddendale, the cluster of buildings in this farming hamlet being hidden by trees.

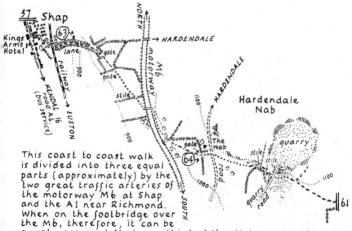

This coast to coast walk is divided into three equal parts (approximately) by the two great traffic arteries of the motorway M6 at Shap and the A1 near Richmond. When on the footbridge over the M6, therefore, it can be smugly assumed that one-third of the distance (as the crow flies) has been covered and rather more in actual mileage because of the indirect passage through Lakeland.

Antiquities of Crosby Ravensworth Fell

HIGH STREET   KIDSTY PIKE   HIGH RAISE

Stone Circle near Oddendale, looking west to Lakeland

Robin Hood's Grave

Erratic boulders:
Granite resting on limestone

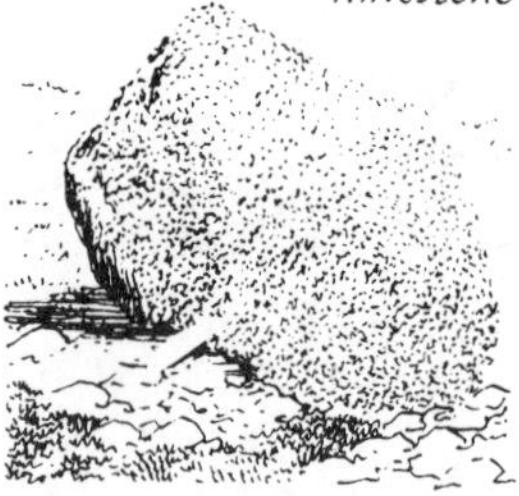

Monument, Black Dub
This bears the following
inscription:

HERE AT BLACK DUB
THE SOURCE OF THE LIVENNET
KING CHARLES THE II
REGALED HIS ARMY
AND DRANK OF THE WATER
ON HIS MARCH FROM SCOTLAND
AUGUST 8 1651

Walkers are requested not to visit to Black Dub monument; the area is a very sensitive one for nature conservation and there is no direct public right of way to the monument from the Coast to Coast route.

Do not disturb the sequestered privacy of the hamlet of Oddendale: keep outside its walls and turn right on a good cart-track rising due south across open ground, making a detour to inspect a stone circle (a double circle) on the right. The track continues to a walled enclosure and barn (Potrigg: a winter pasture screened by trees), and then descends slightly to a depression which cross half-left and climb gently to a stake on the skyline indicating a tumulus, crossing a Roman Road on the way. Keep on, more southerly, passing a low limestone scar and a big granite boulder and sloping down to the shallow valley of Lyvennet Beck. Across this, a distinct track soon forms, with a wall on the left, passing over a slight rise and descending to cross a little valley (streambed usually dry), continuing thence to another dry valley. Here, 150 yards up from the wall, is the ancient cairn of Robin Hood's Grave.

Surprisingly, the hamlet of Oddendale is not named on 2½" Ordnance Survey maps, although the small barn of Potrigg is.

The ancient dyke is believed to be the boundary of a former deer park

For the distinct and continuous path alongside the wall we are indebted to many generations of sheep.

Crosby Ravensworth Fell

Crosby Ravensworth today is the quietest of villages and its serenity is profound, but in primitive times it centred a community of some importance, the surrounding countryside being colonised on a rough social pattern, as is evidenced by the plentiful remains of earthworks. The Romans, too, built their road from Low Borrow Bridge to Brougham through here.

*There is no public right of way on the section of the walk from Mile no. 66 to Robin Hood's Grave but the landowner has agreed to allow walkers to continue using the route on a permissive basis. The area is important for nature conservation so dogs should be kept under very close control.

From Robin Hood's Grave (which is not the grave of Robin Hood) return to and accompany the wall until it turns sharp left, when keep on ahead to reach the Crosby Ravensworth road in the vicinity of an active quarry. Bear right then left around a wall-corner to enter a well-defined dry valley that peters out at the junction of the Appleby and Crosby Ravensworth roads.

There is no public right of way on the section of walk from Robin Hood's Grave to the cattle grid after Mile no. 69, but the landowner has agreed to allow walkers to continue using the route on a permissive basis. Please ensure that dogs are kept under very close control as the area is important for nature conservation.

Cross the cattle grid and bear left along a grassy track with a wall on the left. Just after passing a well-preserved lime kiln bear right along a fainter track passing between two walls. Go through the gate ahead, and keep to the left-hand side of the field until you come to the drive of Broadfell Farm. Turn left here, and left again in a quarter of a mile into Street Lane, a traffic-free lane with grass growing down its centre. As soon as the third farm (Scarside) is passed, go through a gate and follow a fence half-left to a wall. Fifty yards along the wall a stile gives access to Knott Lane. The route continues over the stile directly opposite, but a few yards along the lane to the right there is a view through a gateway on the left of the prehistoric stone circle known locally as the Druidical Temple. It is made up entirely of erratic boulders brought to this area by glaciers.

Snacks and refreshments are available in the village of Orton which may be reached by the B.6260 with its superb views of the Howgill Fells, or by the delightful bridleway through Broadfell Farm.

Page revised 1994.

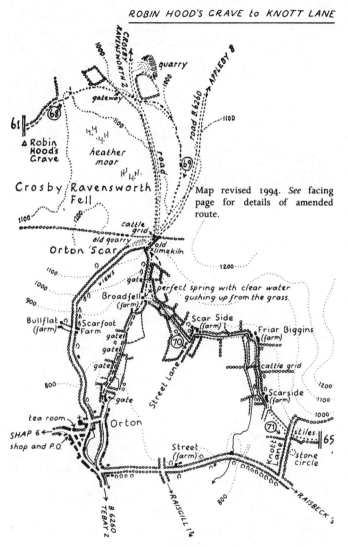

Map revised 1994. *See* facing page for details of amended route.

Sunbiggin Tarn, with the major spring in the foreground

Sunbiggin Tarn

Sunbiggin Tarn has many regular visitors, but none of them would describe it as visually attractive: it is little more than a large reedy pond in the middle of a morass. Its attractions lie in other directions, mainly as a haunt and nesting-place of water-fowl in variety — this is a rewarding 'station' for birdwatchers. Botanists too find delight on the limestone banks nearby. It is a suntrap and, thanks (or otherwise) to the public road alongside, a popular picnic-place. The geology is also interesting: note how the limestone below the road ends abruptly along a line where many springs bubble to the surface; the tarn itself, of course, occupies a basin of impermeable rock.

Rayseat Pike Long Barrow

The barrow from the south

The long barrow on Rayseat Pike is one of the best relics of its kind and possibly the earliest evidence of the prehistory of Westmorland. It was excavated, examined and measured in 1875, the search revealing the remains of both adults and children. An unexpected discovery was a cremation trench containing many burnt bones, a feature that has caused speculation as to the age of this ancient burial ground. The dimensions of the barrow were ascertained as 179 feet in length with a width tapering from 62 feet to 36 feet.

Rayseat Pike is a feature which appears on Wainwright's original route, but this was not on a public right of way and the route has now been revised, see facing page

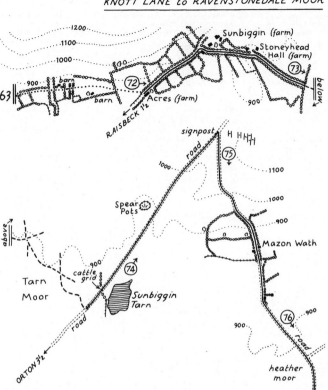

When the wall comes to an end aim for a clump of trees ahead, and then for another clump of trees that marks the farmstead of Acres. Turn left here into a country lane, and continue along the lane when it becomes unmetalled at the last farm. Before long the pastures are left behind, and the route crosses the heather-clad waste of Tarn Moor. Turn right at the crossways, ignore a path bearing right, and turn right at another crossways to an unfenced road. Turn left here, passing Sunbiggin Tarn on the right. In just over a mile turn right onto another unfenced road, and in a mile and a half turn left at the second cattle grid. The route is now a mile longer than it was originally.

Whole page amended 1994

Severals Village Settlement

The Royal Commission on Ancient Monuments included in their inventory for Westmorland (1935) references to a complex of prehistoric villages, comprising stone-walled fields, hutments, dykes and pathways, on the south-east slope of the fellside above Smardale, describing this as a key site and one of the most remarkable in Britain.

These enthusiastic references lead a visitor to expect more than there is in fact to be seen, at least by inexpert eyes: indeed a man with other matters on his mind could walk across the site without noticing any features out of the ordinary, while a man of greater observation may be vaguely puzzled to see the ground apparently divided by low embankments into compartments but probably attach no importance or significance to this fragmentary evidence of past use of the land. To trained eyes, however, there is a story to be learnt from these primitive earthworks: the parapets are the foundations of former walls, marking boundaries and enclosing fields, the sunken ways were farm tracks, the small patterned areas are the traces of stone huts. Men lived here, as a community, where no men now live and few men ever come: the site is very remote and today rarely visited.

It is a place that would be better appreciated from an aerial view than a tour of the ground. The site has never been excavated; if it were to be a gap in our knowledge of the early settlers in the district might well be bridged.

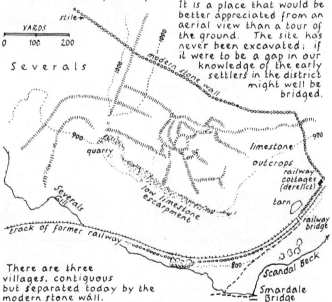

There are three villages, contiguous but separated today by the modern stone wall.

From the cattle grid there follows a long mile of fast walking with splendid views of Mallerstang Edge, Wild Boar Fell and the Howgill Fells forward and to the right. Beyond Bents Farm a gate in the intake wall is reached near a sheepfold. This gate gives access to a large pasture and offers a direct continuation of the route but there is no 'official' footpath through it: the only legitimate entrance is another gate half a mile further along the wall. The route mileage assumes that the first gate is used, the farmer's blessing having been obtained (or taken for granted) but conscientious walkers who would no more commit a trespass than a murder must use the second gate at the cost of an extra mile's walking. Whichever is used, watch carefully for the stile in the crosswall shown on the map: without its help the wall cannot be negotiated. Now cross the low ridge, along the crest of which the first earthwork (the remains of the western boundary wall) of the ancient village settlement is met, and go downhill to the Smardale valley ahead across the settlement.

*

Use a gate near the barn at the bottom of the field to cross the old railway track by a bridge and turn to the right to descend to Smardale Bridge in an area of prehistoric remains. Sunlight clearly defines

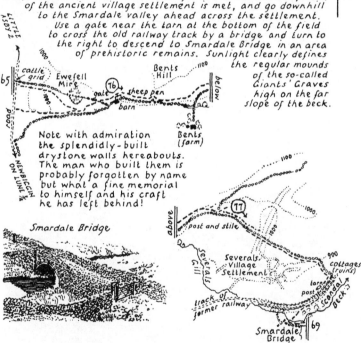

the regular mounds
of the so-called
Giants' Graves
high on the far
slope of the beck.

Note with admiration the splendidly-built drystone walls hereabouts. The man who built them is probably forgotten by name but what a fine memorial to himself and his craft he has left behind!

Smardale Bridge

*The new map at the foot of this page (amended 1994) shows the revised route to be taken across Severals Settlement. There is no public right of way here but the landowner has generously agreed to allow walkers to use the route on a permissive basis subject to a realignment for conservation purposes. For this reason, please be sure to remain on the waymarked path.

Giants' Graves, Smardale Bridge

In the vicinity of Smardale Bridge are many raised mounds, rectangular in plan, about 15 yards long and 5 yards wide, and obviously not natural formations. They are indicated on Ordnance maps as 'Giants Graves' —the name attributed to them by local informants at the time of the first survey; their origin, however, was unknown.

The purpose of these 'pillow mounds' is still obscure, the only certain thing being that they are not graves of giants. Similar ancient mounds in other parts of the country have been identified as warrens made by man to facilitate the breeding and capture of rabbits, but here, in Smardale, this explanation is unlikely to apply, for their proximity to the village settlements strongly suggests an association. Rabbits were not introduced to this country until after the 11th century but the settlements (and mounds) almost certainly date back to the dawn of history. The mounds have the appearance of long barrows or burial sites — but this possibility is discounted by the best authorities, who seem more prepared to accept the theory, pending verification, that they may well have been constructed as platforms for stacking bracken.

There is a field of enquiry waiting near Smardale Bridge for an archaeologist with a spade.

Smardale

with two giants' graves in the foreground

SMARDALE BRIDGE to LIMEKILN HILL

Cross Smardale Bridge and continue uphill on a cart-track between walls. From a gate on the left, after 200 yards, there is a good view of Smardale Gill and the railway viaduct. At a bend in the wall beyond a gate in a fence there is a close view, over the wall, of two of the 'giants' graves' so numerous in this locality. Further, a gate in a crosswall at a sheepfold admits to the large open moorland of Smardale Fell, where a distinct path, used by tractors, goes forward over the crest of a minor undulation with a curiously narrow enclosure a mile long on the left and a small cairned summit on the right. The walking now is excellent, amongst intermittent heather and limestone outcrops. When the wall trends away left, a branch path follows it down to Smardale Hall: ignore this, and keep on forward over another undulation, now with a fine view ahead across the valley of the River Eden to Nine Standards Rigg, Mallerstang Edge and the long high skyline of the Pennines — the next stage of the journey. A wall is met and accompanied downhill, crossing a muddy patch and passing two old limekilns, the first near-perfect, the second collapsed.

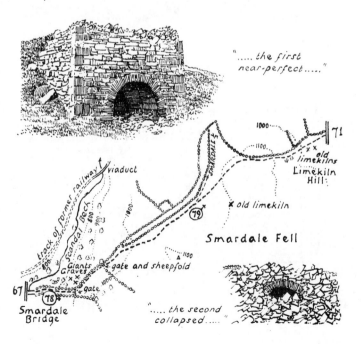

" ..... the first near-perfect ....."

1000
1100
71
x x old limekilns
Limekiln Hill

track of former railway
viaduct
SMARDALE GILL
Standal Beck
800
x old limekiln
79
Smardale Fell
1100
Giants Graves
gate and sheepfold
67
78
gate
Smardale Bridge

" ..... the second collapsed ....."

Village Settlements, Waitby

After leaving the Waitby road, the route crosses a pasture that has obvious traces of the earthworks of an old settlement, then passes under the railway bridge to another field, where, immediately on the right amongst scattered hawthorns, are the equally distinct evidences of two other settlements, the southern parts of which were destroyed during the construction of the railway except for sections still visible on the other side. All these remains, consisting mainly of raised parapets, are easily traced and reveal irregular enclosures and hut circles.

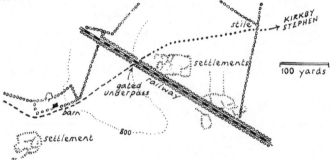

Kirkby Stephen

Kirkby Stephen is an obvious staging-post on the walk, a place for licking wounds and replenishing supplies. Here are shops and cafés galore, many hotels, a youth hostel and much private accommodation. Although but a small town of less than 2000 population it is in fact the largest community so far met on the walk, and in the distance remaining to be travelled only Richmond offers comparable facilities.

It is the market town for a wide rural area and therefore is a busy little place, yet it is away from main tourist routes and remains unspoiled. The A.685 running through it carries traffic between the north-east and the Lancashire coast and comes to life when the Blackpool 'lights' are 'on'. There is a variety of religious establishments, the principal being the Parish Church of St Stephen, and this and other buildings in and around the Market Place have interesting features.

The town has length but little width. It hugs the A.685 for a mile almost without built-up offshoots. Unseen from the main thoroughfare but confining the town on the east is the River Eden, not far travelled from its source in the hills of Mallerstang but already a considerable watercourse. It goes on to enter the Solway Firth near Carlisle.

At a gate a minor road (to Smardale) is reached. Formerly a footpath crossed the field directly opposite, but this has now been closed. Instead, walk right along the road to a junction where turn left down the Waitby road, leaving it at the second (not the first) gate on the right to descend a pasture between a barn on the left and the earthworks of an ancient settlement on the right to an underpass on the railway ahead (this is the Settle to Carlisle line), beyond which, in the next field, are traces of more settlements. A stile in the far corner (east) admits to a large pasture. A path is found near a line of limestone outcrops and passes down a shallow valley, inclining right to a stile in a wall near a clump of larch trees. From this go down a field past a barn to a gate and stile at the bottom. Ahead, two underpasses in quick succession lead beneath the two branches of a disused railway to the muddy environs of Green Riggs farm, bypassed by * two gates on the left (or, more easily, go through the farmyard), so joining a lane that leads in a short mile alongside the flat-topped hill of Croglam Castle (not worth a detour) to Kirkby Stephen. The lane becomes a back street for houses on the main road A.685, which can be joined at the first tarmac link. (where there is a primitive 'Gents'), ** emerging almost opposite the Youth Hostel. Turn left for the town centre.

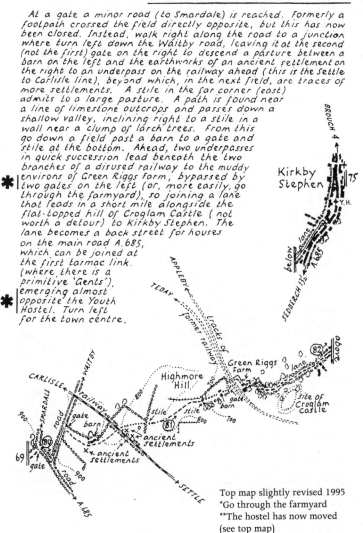

Top map slightly revised 1995
*Go through the farmyard
**The hostel has now moved
(see top map)

SECTION MAP : *KIRKBY STEPHEN to KELD* : 12¾ miles

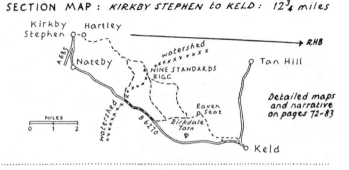

Detailed maps and narrative on pages 72-83

This section has an important significance : on the top of Nine Standards Rigg the main Pennine watershed is crossed and Yorkshire entered. Thus far, all rivers and streams met have flowed to join the Irish Sea, west; beyond, they all flow to the North Sea, east. Thus far we have travelled *against* the grain, so to speak, but from here onwards we walk *with* the watercourses and to the same destination — but this doesn't mean it's now downhill all the way or that we have reached the halfway mark. Nevertheless, a quiet celebration on Nine Standards would not be out of place : at least there is no higher ground ahead on the journey.

At Keld we reach one of the major Yorkshire dales and the finest, Swaledale. Here too we collide, briefly, with the Pennine Way. Keld, famous for its waterfalls, is a small hamlet, a real outpost in the hills, but accommodation is restricted to a youth hostel and a few cottages.

The route recommended, over Nine Standards, traverses wild country, much of it pathless and without landmarks, and is not suitable for a wet or misty day. If there is a need to proceed regardless of bad weather, the quiet fell road leaving Nateby for Keld should be used instead : it is a motor road (B.6270) but is almost traffic free except on summer Sundays. It reaches a height of 1698'. Note that in the event of the onset of bad weather on the Nine Standards route this road can be joined anywhere simply by walking south : it is unenclosed by fences across the top. It should also be borne in mind that, conversely, if the weather improves after a bad start, Nine Standards can be reached quickly from the summit of the road.

The B.6270 is the sort of road, lonely and inhospitable, no more than a narrow thread of tarmac through barren hills, where a passing motorist feels an obligation to offer a lift to a solitary walker, especially one who seems inherently decent and is bravely struggling against the elements. If this happens you will decline, of course.

Section map revised 1994.

Kirkby Stephen

top:
The Parish Church
of St. Stephen

bottom:
Frank's Bridge.

Hartley

Leave Kirkby Stephen at the market place, taking a byway east to an old footbridge (Franks Bridge) over the River Eden, where a path turns right along the bank (ignore a branch to Nateby). A rising field and a short lane lead to Hartley, a charming village threaded by a stream and adorned with fine trees. Cross a wooden footbridge to the road and follow this to the right, uphill, passing vast limeworks and quarries, to its end after 1½ miles at a signpost pointing the bridleway to Nine Standards, which follow. The views from the road are good and progress along it is fast.

In the first impression of this book an alternative route from Hartley to the bridleway signpost at 1100' was suggested (but not recommended), following a path indicated on Ordnance maps.   PLEASE NOTE THAT THIS FOOTPATH IS <u>NOT</u> A RIGHT OF WAY.

Annoyance has been caused by walkers using this alternative, which lies entirely on STRICTLY PRIVATE FARMLAND, and the map below has been amended to exclude it.   From Hartley, PLEASE KEEP TO THE TARMAC FELL ROAD.

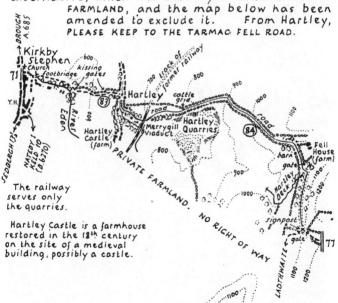

The railway serves only the quarries.

Hartley Castle is a farmhouse restored in the 18th century on the site of a medieval building, possibly a castle.

Birkett Hill looks aggressively attractive!

There are many theories about the origin of the group of cairns long known as the Nine Standards, as is usually the case when the truth is not known. Certainly they are very old, appearing on 18th century maps and giving their name to the hill they adorn. They have multiplied slowly, visitors in more recent times having added a few more.

Nine Standards

They occupy a commanding position overlooking the Eden valley, this giving rise to the legend that they were built to give the marauding Scots the impression that an English army was encamped here. More likely they were boundary cairns (the county boundary formerly passed through them), or beacons. Harder to believe is the theory that the builders were local lads with nothing better to do to pass their time. Whatever their purpose, they were meant to endure, having suffered little from the storms of centuries.

The attainment of Nine Standards Rigg is an occasion for celebration. This is the main watershed of the walk and the most extensive and interesting viewpoint on it. Far back in the west is the skyline of Lakeland; the massifs of Cross Fell and Mickle Fell form the northern horizon, buttressing many miles of the Eden valley; in the south, much nearer, are the hills of Mallerstang and southeast is the promised land of Swaledale, fading into the haze of distance between the lofty portals of Great Shunner Fell and Rogan's Seat. Somewhere in that haze is the foot of our personal rainbow, journey's end.
  If you are carrying a can of beer prepare to drink it now.

Erosion in the area around Nine Standards and Nine Standards Rigg has become severe, and the Yorkshire Dales National Park Authority has designated seasonal routes, details of which follow on pages 77–81.

Important: first read the note at the top of page 78.

For the Red and Blue Routes: Having crossed Hartley Fell on a good bridleway, bear left at the signpost at 1600 feet and pass along a grassy track curving through a cleft in the hills and waymarked by small cairns. Ignore a path to the left just past a prominent cairn and continue uphill to the Nine Standards. The summit of Nine Standards Rigg is then within easy reach a few minutes away.

For the Green Route: bear right at the signpost at 1600 feet and follow the bridleway, at first alongside a wall, to 1800 feet; turn right at a Coast to Coast signpost towards a wind shelter. *Continued below right.*

Rigg Beck forms a deep valley on the right. At its head the stream is subterranean as it enters a limestone canyon, well known to local botanists as the habitat of many flowers and mosses.

Tailbrigg Pots mark a pronounced division between limestone (west) and gritstone peat (east). Keep to limestone for better progress.

This map is extended southwards to show the **Green Route** which runs south to the top of the Nateby–Keld road.

The Green Route *continued from above*: From the wind shelter, the path ahead can be seen passing to the left of a walled enclosure. The path continues past the Tailbrigg Pots to reach the B6270, where a left turn should be made.

Map amended 1998.

To minimise erosion in the area of Nine Standards Rigg, it has been necessary to ask walkers to use different routes at different seasons of the year. These routes are signposted from Hartley Fell to Raven Seat. **The Green Route/December to April** avoids the Nine Standards altogether; **the Red Route/May to July** is the original route via White Mossy Hill; **the Blue Route/August to November** descends from Nine Standards Rigg into Whitsundale. The start of each of these routes is found on page 77.

Whitsundale

The valley of Whitsundale bisects an upland wilderness east of Nine Standards Rigg and winds its way down into the lower reaches of Birkdale. It is of considerable size yet little known and rarely visited: it is deeply enclosed by moors, is unseen from usual pedestrian tracks and unsuspected from the only motor road in the vicinity. A few farms occupy the entrance to the valley but beyond Raven Seat all is desolation profound.

The pillar on
Millstones

From December to April/Green Route: Follow the B6270 for just over 1½ miles, then take an unmetalled road to the left. Follow this and by the time you reach the shooting hut you will have joined up with the Red Route (*see* facing page).

Please see copy opposite.

Map revised 1998. From the Nine Standards Rigg aim for the smooth grassy rise of White Mossy Hill, slightly east of south. From **August to November/Blue Route** turn left at the signpost in the depression and follow a line of posts to the east. From **May to July/Red Route**, keep straight on at the signpost for two miles, passing (after about a mile) a well-constructed pillar on the edge of the sloping plateau. When the path meets an unmetalled road, turn left and shortly pass a shooting hut. Then continue along the valley of Ney Gill to the east.

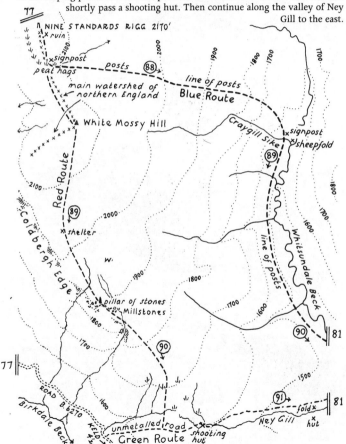

For details of the **Green Route/December to April** *see* foot of facing page.

Raven Seat   route ----

Road bridge,
Raven Seat

Waterfall,
Whitsundale
Beck

See map top p.81
**The Blue Route/
August–November**
leaves the beck at a
wall and turns south.
It joins the other two
routes at a ruined
barn just above Ney
Gill.

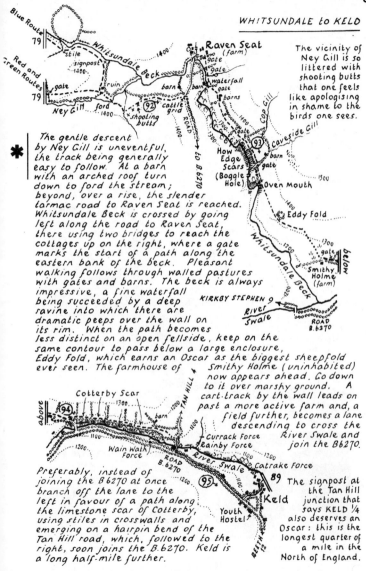

The vicinity of Ney Gill is so littered with shooting butts that one feels like apologising in shame to the birds one sees.

* The gentle descent by Ney Gill is uneventful, the track being generally easy to follow. At a barn with an arched roof turn down to ford the stream; beyond, over a rise, the slender tarmac road to Raven Seat is reached. Whitsundale Beck is crossed by going left along the road to Raven Seat, there using two bridges to reach the cottages up on the right, where a gate marks the start of a path along the eastern bank of the beck. Pleasant walking follows through walled pastures with gates and barns. The beck is always impressive, a fine waterfall being succeeded by a deep ravine into which there are dramatic peeps over the wall on its rim. When the path becomes less distinct on an open fellside, keep on the same contour to pass below a large enclosure, Eddy Fold, which earns an Oscar as the biggest sheepfold ever seen. The farmhouse of Smithy Holme (uninhabited) now appears ahead. Go down to it over marshy ground. A cart-track by the wall leads on past a more active farm and, a field further, becomes a lane descending to cross the River Swale and join the B6270.

Preferably, instead of joining the B6270 at once branch off the lane to the left in favour of a path along the limestone scar of Cotterby, using stiles in crosswalls and emerging on a hairpin bend of the Tan Hill road, which, followed to the right, soon joins the B.6270. Keld is a long half-mile further.

The signpost at the Tan Hill junction that says KELD ¼ also deserves an Oscar: this is the longest quarter of a mile in the North of England.

*Map revised 1998; see foot of facing page for details of the **Blue Route**.

82

Keld.......

The little cluster of stone buildings at Keld, tidily yet haphazardly arranged along its only 'street', is attractively situated on a headland overlooking the Swale. Little has changed here for generations past, and proud dates and names of proud men adorn the doorways and walls and even the chapel belfry: a sundial records the hours but time is measured in centuries at Keld. This is the end of Swaledale —beyond are the wild moors of the watershed.

Cottages, farmsteads and innumerable barns starkly stand against a bleak and barren background. The joy of Keld is the Swale, a swift-flowing torrent sheltered by white cliffs of limestone fringed with trees and broken by falls and cataracts on its fast course from the desolate hills to the soft pastures of the valley.

Always, at Keld, there is the music of the river.

.... and some of its waterfalls

Wain Wath Force

KELD IS HALFWAY!

Catrake Force

East Gill Force

Kisdon Force

SECTION MAP : *KELD to REETH* : 11¼ miles

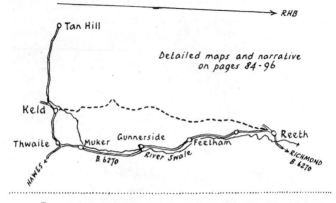

Detailed maps and narrative
on pages 84-96

For most walkers the royal road from Keld to Reeth will always be along the lovely banks of the Swale, the first three miles to Muker especially being very beautiful and the whole distance with minor interruptions being possible by using public footpaths on or near the riverside. If the day be wet or misty this is the way to go.

But the high-level route recommended in the following pages is of infinitely greater interest in addition to providing an excellent moorland walk made easy by the use of miners' tracks. The sites of several of the abandoned Swaledale lead mines are visited on the way, and, although they are now ruinous, enough remains to enable the imaginative visitor to reconstruct the scene as it used to be when thousands of men toiled here. They left their mark, and it is a dirty mark, so expect little of beauty in this section.

It is in this part of the walk, as our route aims from the hills for the valleys, that we pass from the settlements of the early Viking raiders, who found, in the mountainous northwest, country to their liking, a 'home from home', to those of the Danes, Angles and Saxons, who preferred the richer low ground to which, as tillers of the soil, they were accustomed.

It is almost possible to fix a boundary between the two types of settlement by reference to placenames only. *Keld* and *Thwaite* are pure Norse, as are the names of many natural features: *gill, fell, foss;* but as we proceed east to the gentler middle reaches of the valley, placenames ending in *-ton* (Grinton, Fremington) become frequent and are indicative of the Anglo-Saxon occupation, of which indeed there are visual evidences also in the terraced fields or lynchets seen here but absent in the uncultivated upper valley, where the Norsemen used the ground mainly for grazing. Earlier still were the Brigantes, who have also left their traces on the landscape. A few embossed pigs of lead have told of the Romans' interest in Swaledale, while an ancient fortification near Reeth dates back to prehistoric times. Over the ages Swaledale has been quite cosmopolitan; a new influx of 'offcomers' is today acquiring its old barns and cottages for leisure pursuits. The natives remain impassive. They are accustomed to foreigners in Swaledale.

The route from Keld at once heads deep into the moors at Swinner Gill, from which it traverses high land to descend into Gunnerside Gill, a lonely graveyard of industrial relics, thence crossing a moorland devastated by spoil (where a secondary industry, of winning gravel, is now operating), after which it descends again to another mining area, and then skirts a more friendly fellside to reach Reeth, a pleasant and hospitable village with a choice of good hotels and private accommodation. There is a youth hostel across the river at nearby Grinton.... Reeth welcomes all, irrespective of nationality!

A small but excellent publication recommended for supplementary reading is
SWALEDALE. by Ron and Lucie Hinson
(*Dalesman Publishing Co.Ltd*)

For a deeper study of the history of Swaledale, its landscape and geology, mining industry and various facets of its life and times, the writings of Dr. Arthur Raistrick provide a wealth of authoritative material. Much of his work is published in booklet form by the ~~Dalesman~~ *Publishing Co. Ltd.*

Lead Mining in Swaledale

In a search for information relating to the life and happenings of centuries ago one must often rely on imagination to fill in the details from the scanty evidences still remaining.

Not so in Swaledale. Anyone who wanders up the moors from the valley soon finds himself in the midst of a graphic scene of industrial decay that simply cannot be passed unnoticed. The gills, the fellsides, even the summits, have been torn asunder; shafts and levels pierce the earth like pockmarks; petrified rivers of stone litter the steep slopes; barren gullies make big scars in the heather; the skeletons of abandoned and derelict buildings stand gaunt and grey amid a chaos of spoil heaps. An observer of this dismal wreckage is left in no doubt that Swaledale has a long history of mining — and that this history has come to a full stop.

The date of the mines is uncertain. Most of them were opened in the 17th and 18th centuries but it is known that the Romans extracted lead here, probably from mines already existing, and that the Yorkshire monasteries owned workings. Later, a free-for-all developed, the landowners and men individually and in groups plundering the hills in search of profitable veins of ore. Another Klondyke arose in these wild hills. Thousands of men were engaged: a few 'struck it rich' but most toiled for little reward. Then, over the space of a decade towards the end of the 19th century, the industry collapsed. Not only were the best veins worked out but cheap foreign imports supplied the home demand. The population of Swaledale fell dramatically. Lead mining gave way to farming as the valley's source of prosperity.

In the triangle of land between Swaledale and Arkengarthdale particularly the scene even today is one of sterile devastation, despoliation, decay... There is no beauty in these sorry ruins but a great fascination for those of imagination who can picture in their minds the scene as it was a century before and still more for those who have the knowledge to piece together the fragments that remain.

There is a great need, before everything crumbles to dust, to preserve at least one of the mines as a site museum, not necessarily restoring the smelt and crushing mills and opening up the levels but reclaiming enough to demonstrate the methods of operation and the tools and equipment used, with a plan of the workings, graphs of annual output, and such supporting documentary records as may still be available. This could perhaps be done by one of the Universities or archaeological groups, and should be financed from Government funds.

Our route takes us through the heart of the lead mining district yet gives only a faint insight of the vast area explored and exploited for ore. But note especially the Blakethwaite and Old Gang workings, which we pass, either one of which could be adapted for 20th century study and, it might well be hoped, for 20th century appreciation of the initiative, industry and ingenuity of men who lived hard, in times less favoured than those of today.

We have lost too much of the past through concern for the present.

PRINCIPAL MINING AREAS IN SWALEDALE

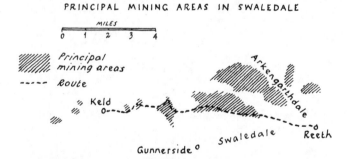

This diagram indicates roughly the main areas extensively mined for lead, but in addition countless old shafts and levels, many of which proved abortive and were not fully developed, occur everywhere on the moors. The triangle of high ground between Arkengarthdale and Swaledale proved the most productive area, several square miles here being intensively worked — as is testified by today's sad scenery.

88

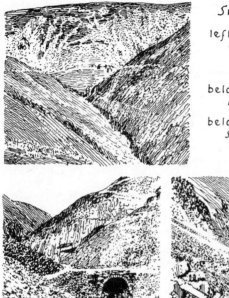

Swinner Gill

left:
   the approach

below left:
   the bridge

below right:
   Swinnergill Kirk

right:
   the ruins of the
   smelt mill, the
   waterfall, and
   the mine level
   at the foot of
   East Grain

KELD to SWINNERGILL MINES

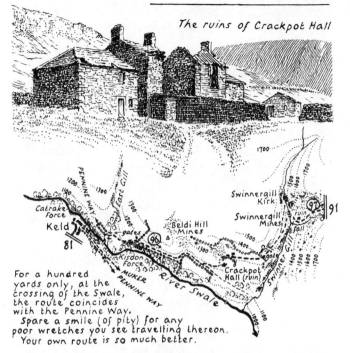

The ruins of Crackpot Hall

For a hundred
yards only, at the
crossing of the Swale,
the route coincides
with the Pennine Way.
 Spare a smile (of pity) for any
poor wretches you see travelling thereon.
 Your own route is so much better.

Leave Keld by the signposted lane (to Kisdon Force and to
Muker) opposite the post office. After 300 muddy yards a path
indicated by a Pennine Way signpost turns down left to reach a
footbridge over the Swale, which cross and ascend the field
opposite to a bridge above East Gill Force, in charming scenery.
Here the Pennine Way turns left, our own route going across
the gated bridge and continuing on a good cart-track to the
sad ruins of Crackpot Hall, a once-handsome farmhouse (with
a lovely view downriver to Muker) abandoned due to mining
subsidence. Skirt the wall behind the ruins, passing a barn on
another good track to arrive at a gate with an imposing view
forward. Now a narrower path descends slightly, high above the
deep rift of Swinner Gill, and, ignoring a branch left, reaches a
fine bridge and the ruins of a smelting mill on the far bank,
near a conspicuous waterfall with a mine-level adjacent. At
this point Swinner Gill is left in favour of the branch-valley
coming down from the east (East Grain), where a thin track
ascends roughly along its north bank.

Blakethwaite Smelt Mill

right:
North Hush,
from
Bunton Hush

below:
Gunnerside Gill

SWINNERGILL MINES to GUNNERSIDE MINES

What is a hush?

A hush, in mining terms, is a ravine contrived by prospectors on a steep slope and is caused by the sudden release of water artificially dammed above it in such force as to strip the vegetation and scour the ground with the object of revealing any mineral content in the subsoil that might indicate the presence of a vein. (Today a bulldozer would be used). These hushes are found in many mining districts and are especially conspicuous in Gunnerside Gill.

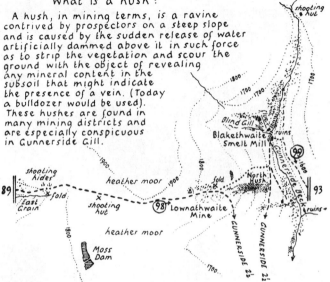

When the gradient alongside East Grain eases, the track becomes indistinct on wet ground near a sheepfold but the way ahead is clear on emerging from a bed of rushes. As it crosses the top of the moor, the track rapidly improves to first-class standard, especially beyond a shooting hut, which, as the ruts indicate, is obviously serviced from the east. The walking here, on a grass ribbon flanked by dark heather moorland, is excellent, with no danger of straying off course and far-reaching views to be enjoyed. At the highest point (1895') there is a glimpse of Moss Dam, an interesting relic of mining days crossed by a causeway. As the track descends a cairn on the left marks the start of an area of mining debris, and, beyond a sheepfold, a great disturbance of the ground ahead indicates the natural but man-inspired ravine of North Hush. Here the track turns to the right (for Gunnerside); leave it now and go down the pathless heather on the north side of the hush to reach a good track below, turning left along this to the imposing remains of the Blakethwaite Smelt Mill, where the beck is crossed by a huge stone slab to a cloister-like ruin with a fine arched entrance. Looking back, note the flue coming straight down the rough fellside from a notch in the skyline and the well-preserved kiln to its right. Now scramble up steep grass to a green path and follow it to the right.

Level House Bridge

Old Gang
Smelt Mill

GUNNERSIDE MINES to SURRENDER BRIDGE

The path along the east bank of Gunnerside Beck arrives
suddenly at a remarkable area of devastation, a succession
of hushes having gouged out much of the fellside ahead. Do
not descend with the path to the plentiful remains of mining
activity in the bottom of the gill but slant half-left over
the stony wastes, climbing steadily across to the farthest
hush, which ascend to open slopes above with a broken wall
on the right, where, near a sheepfold, a track from Gunnerside
is joined. Now follows a surprising tract of ground: on the
top of the moor ahead all vegetation has been destroyed by
a deep covering of gravel, the spoil of old mines and pits.
Although the altitude reaches 1863', nothing
less like a Yorkshire moor can be imagined.

100 miles!
Yippee!!

Old Gang Mines

For a third of a mile not a blade of grass nor a
sprig of heather is seen, the natural moorland
having been transformed into an arid desert of
stone. The spoil here is being reclaimed, and,
incongruously, tractors may be met. Whether
or not one approves of the ravaging of natural
scenery on so vast a scale, the access roadway for
vehicles leading down to the valley ahead is a great
boon for foot-travellers, who can make rapid
progress along it and are spared the slow
and wearying trudge over rough ground
to which they would be committed
without its help. On the descent,
if the day be clear, there is a
first glimpse of the
Cleveland Hills
far ahead.

Old Gang
Smelt Mill

The vehicle roadway
descends easily to a bridge
and continues down the valley,
passing an interesting group of
mine buildings and a mill chimney.
If not delayed by inspections of these
relics, Surrender Bridge will be reached
in fine style at a speed of four m.p.h.

Surrender
Bridge

A: to FLETHAM
B: to HEALAUGH

Smelt Mill, Surrender Bridge

Calver Hill

Cross the tarmac just above Surrender Bridge and continue on a signposted 'public footpath' downstream to the sad ruin of a smelt mill. Here bear half-left across a heather moor, wet in places. There is no path, but aim for the left edge of a green field seen ahead.

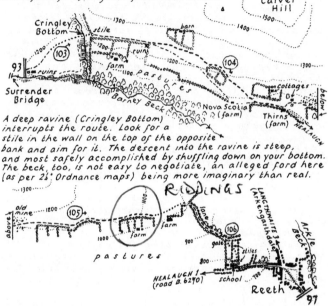

A deep ravine (Cringley Bottom) interrupts the route. Look for a stile in the wall on the top of the opposite bank and aim for it. The descent into the ravine is steep, and most safely accomplished by shuffling down on your bottom. The beck, too, is not easy to negotiate, an alleged ford here (as per 2½" Ordnance maps) being more imaginary than real.

Scramble up the grassy east bank to the stile (found near a junction of walls): it is of the narrow 'squeeze through' type and will pose a grave problem for walkers with bow legs. But thenceforward all is plain sailing on an enjoyable 'high-level' path. From the stile keep above the intake wall to a ruinous barn, where take the higher of two paths on the open moor: it matures into a cart-track and slants down to a farm, Thirns. Here turn briefly uphill, left, to pass in front of a cottage, Moorcock, and follow a good track through an area of spoil (the site of an old mine), continuing forward above intake walls on the same contour until a farm appears ahead. This is avoided by crossing open ground well to its left, rounding a wall-corner and entering a gated lane that descends between walls to the B.6270, the last section being short-cut in fields to reach the road by a ginnel alongside a school. Turn left to Reeth. The views in the course of this walk are excellent.

Reeth

Reeth, as befits its proud title as the 'capital' of upper Swaledale, occupies a strategic point of vantage on an open hillside overlooking the confluence of Arkle Beck and the Swale. Here the deep trench of Arkengarthdale, which seems destined to bear forever the gaunt scars of its abandoned mining industry, loses its identity in the more verdant and lovelier main valley.

Reeth is a pleasant place, its buildings forming a square around a large green that is gay with daffodils in springtime but littered on summer weekends with coaches and cars and too many human beings. Once primarily concerned with mining and housing twice its present population Reeth today is mainly engaged in catering for a growing influx of tourists and supplying the needs of the valley communities: there are many hotels and shops. Notably absent from the scene is the parish church: this, 'the cathedral of Swaledale', is situated a mile away across the River Swale at Grinton. Reeth is, in fact, distant from the river, and is more intimately concerned with Arkle Beck, itself a considerable watercourse, which forms the eastern boundary of the village.

No railway ever penetrated the upper reaches of Swaledale — what a scenic journey it would have provided, what a pageant of beauty! — but a few buses pass through Reeth daily, linking Richmond and Keld.

A corner of Reeth

SECTION MAP : REETH to RICHMOND : 10½ miles

→ RHB

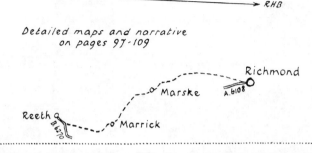

Detailed maps and narrative
on pages 97-109

Richmond

o Marske
A.6108

Reeth o
B.6270

o Marrick

This section is short and easily accomplished, but is so abundantly endowed with variety and beauty and interest that it would be unforgivable to rush it in half a day; one should arrange nevertheless to finish with an hour or two to spare for an inspection of Richmond's many historical buildings. The scenery throughout this section is of high quality, with the Swale the dominant feature and lovely everywhere. The river may be followed more closely than the route given, but it is preferable to keep high along the hillsides and so enjoy quieter walking and extensive views. This the recommended route does.

REETH to MARRICK PRIORY

Take the Richmond road out of Reeth, leaving it when it turns south at Fremington and continuing along the Marske by-road for a further half-mile to a much-opened gate signposted 'Marrick Priory', which proceed to on a much-trodden farm road in pleasant surroundings, the lovely river and valley scenery being marred only by the presence of caravans. The Swale has grown fat since we last saw it at Keld.

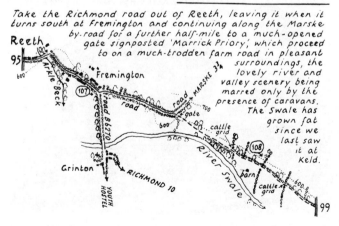

Reeth
95
600

Arkle Beck

Fremington
107
road B.6270
road
road MARSKE 3¾
gate
700
600
cattle grid
108

Grinton
RICHMOND 10
YOUTH HOSTEL

River Swale

barn
cattle grid
600
99

Marrick Priory

Marrick Priory was established in the 12th century and occupied by Benedictine nuns until it was dissolved by Henry VIII. It became a sad ruin except for the tower but some restoration has been undertaken, and new buildings added for use as an adventure centre.

Marrick Priory is in ruins except for the tower, and partly concealed by new buildings occupied by the Ripon Diocese as an adventure centre and the barns and byres of Abbey Farm adjacent. A gate gives access to it.

At this point leave the farm road in favour of a grass path slanting up to a wicket-gate giving entrance into a wood. A flagged path leads upwards alongside a wall: a delightful interlude, the way being edged by floriferous banks. (This path through the wood is reputed to have 375 steps, but they are insignificant, not like a stairway). The path emerges into a field, reaching a gate in a sea of liquid mud ('slutch' to Lancashire folk) and continuing between a chapel and a church that serve as portals to the small hamlet of Marrick beyond and doubtless give an exaggerated impression of the religious fervour of its few inhabitants. Proceed to the far end of the main 'street' (note the quaint sundial on the wall of the last cottage). Here the tarmac turns a corner, heading north: leave it at this point by a short lane on the right to pass a barn and farmhouse, and then, through gates, incline left alongside a hedge to a stile in a stone wall ahead. More walled fields follow: there is no visible path but stiles of the 'squeeze through' type indicate the right of way. The view ahead now opens up considerably, Hutton's Monument being conspicuous on the line of march. The route now descends to Eller Beck, crossing two fences and a farm road and maintaining a beeline indicated by gates and stiles to the house of Ellers, a charming 'conversion' remarkable by its lack of an access road. Pass round the house to a footbridge consisting of a plank and a handrail and, ascending slightly, aim across the next field diagonally to a gate and continue in the same direction through another.

after restoration.....
Ellers

before restoration.....
The Old White Horse Inn
Marrick

Marrick

Nun Cote Nook (farm)

Ellers

Eller Beck

gate

footbridge

stiles

barn

barn

gate

gate

farm road

hurdle

stile

stiles

chapel

church

gate

barns

gate and mud

cattle grid

wicket gate

wicket gate

Marrick Priory

97

109

110

101

*Map revised 1994. After passing the 'quaint sundial', turn right and when the tarmac ends bear left along a track. Keep going straight on, and rejoin the original route when you pass East End Farm.

Marske.........

...Hall

...Church

...Bridge

The path from Ellers reaches the farm road to
Hollins (Hollings on Ordnance maps) alongside
a plantation. The right of way, straight ahead,
is now interrupted by a wire fence, which
can be negotiated by a gate on the right.
Continue alongside a well-built wall (the
boundary of the former deer park of
Marske Hall), crossing the fence again
to a gate on the right, from where a
slanting course across a field leads
to the Reeth-Marske road, reached
by a stile opposite a bungalow. In
splendid scenery, go down the road
to Marske Bridge (between a
memorial garden sanctuary
and the ornamental
grounds of the Hall)
and up the hill
to the hamlet
of Marske.

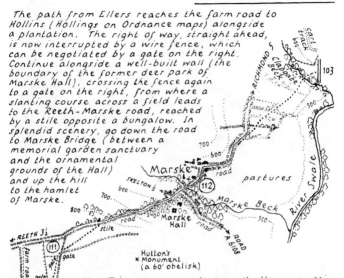

Hutton's
× Monument
(a 60' obelisk)

Hutton's
Monument
marks the
grave of
Matthew
Hutton
(1814)

At a T-junction of roads opposite the post office
take the branch to the right for a third of a mile,
then, on a bend, leave it via a gate on the right,
between trees, which gives access to a public but
invisible path through fields. Aim half-left from
the gate and pass through gaps in three hedges in
succession, then a stile in a fence, and, keeping
in the same direction, reach a footbridge in the
wooded dell of Clapgate Beck. Climb steeply up
the opposite bank, aiming for an electricity pole
between fenced enclosures and passing it to reach
a good cart-track contouring the slope above.

Marske

Marske lies snugly sequestered amongst fine trees in
a side valley of Swaledale, a glacial fold in the hills,
fringed by limestone cliffs with wild heathery moors
beyond. The charm of the place is its natural scenery
but the lovely grounds of Marske Hall contribute to the
richness of the landscape. The Hall was for centuries
the home of the distinguished Hutton family, producing
two Archbishops of York, but is now occupied as flats
following a sale of the estate. Also worthy of mention is
the 12th century church of St. Edmund, retaining some of
its original features and interesting later additions.

High Applegarth
and Whitcliffe Scar

Whitcliffe Wood

The cart-track is the access road for West Applegarth Farm. It occupies a pleasant shelf below a limestone cliff and has a lovely view of the Swale in its wooded valley and of the rolling foothills around Marske, Hutton's Monument being prominent. Go east along it, past an exclusive caravan site and between banks of yew, to the farm, where it ends.   The clue to further progress is the small and solitary barn ahead: go across to it, using a gate adjoining to pass alongside, and, at a stile, enter the pasture beyond.   There is no visible path but three further stiles in stone walls, keeping on the same contour and passing above the farm buildings of Low Applegarth, partly ruinous, point the way to a barn (High Applegarth), whence a track goes forward to join the farm-road serving the last of the Applegarths (East). The scenery hereabouts is pleasant, having the stony slopes of Whitcliffe Scar high on the left— note Willance's Leap on the skyline — and the richly wooded valley of the Swale, its only disfigurement being caravan sites, down on the right.   The way ahead is now distinct, the farm-road entering Whitcliffe Wood bound for Richmond.

Willance's Leap

Whitcliffe Scar and Wood is a popular local walk, the best-known feature being the spot known as Willance's Leap. This is not a spectacular precipice, as the name might suggest, and would attract no attention were it not associated with an occurrence in 1606 when Robert Willance fell down the steep slope here while riding, his horse being killed. Robert was unharmed and, grateful for his deliverance, gave to the town of Richmond as a thankoffering a silver chalice, preserved to this day as one of the town's many treasures.

RICHMOND

MAP OF TOWN CENTRE
AND FEATURES OF INTEREST

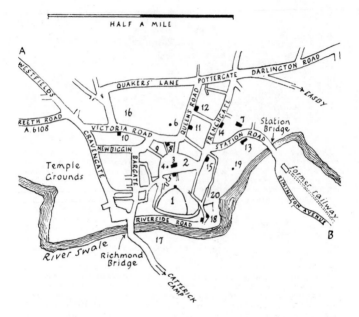

HALF A MILE

1: Castle Ruins	11: General Post Office
2: Market Place	12: Public Library
3: Holy Trinity Church	13: Grammar School
4: Market Cross	14: Council Offices
5: Town Hall	15: R.D.C. Offices
6: Grey Friars' Tower	16: Cricket Ground
7: St. Mary's Parish Church	17: Football Ground
8: Georgian Theatre	18: Gasholders
9: Finkle Street	19: Dogs' Toilet
10: Cinema	20: Waterfalls

A: Point of entry of route into the town
B: Point of departure

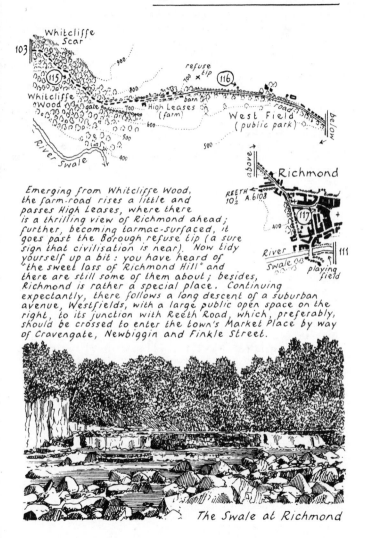

Emerging from Whitcliffe Wood, the farm-road rises a little and passes High Leases, where there is a thrilling view of Richmond ahead; further, becoming tarmac-surfaced, it goes past the Borough refuse tip (a sure sign that civilisation is near). Now tidy yourself up a bit: you have heard of "the sweet lass of Richmond Hill" and there are still some of them about; besides, Richmond is rather a special place. Continuing expectantly, there follows a long descent of a suburban avenue, Westfields, with a large public open space on the right, to its junction with Reeth Road, which, preferably, should be crossed to enter the town's Market Place by way of Cravengate, Newbiggin and Finkle Street.

The Swale at Richmond

Richmond

Richmond is a town unlike others, a place unique, rich in relics of the past, steeped in a long history that still lingers in the ramifications of its castle and the narrow alleys and quaint buildings that huddle in the shelter of the massive Norman keep. The castle, dramatically poised on a cliff high above the Swale, is the dominating feature, but hardly less impressive is the large cobbled market place with the ancient church of the Holy Trinity rising from the stones and having a row of shops beneath its north aisle, or the fine tower standing amid the ruins of a Friary. Other buildings also have associations with days gone by, notably the restored Georgian Theatre. Many of the streets, too, have an atmosphere of antiquity, happily preserved in their names, and picturesque corners abound. It is a town of reminders of times long past. Richmond folk have always jealously guarded their heritage and consequently the town centre shows little in the nature of 20th century 'improvements' (Woolworths being an exception that proves the rule): their reward for vigilance and a recognition of true values is a romantic town that has 'gloriously defied time' and today looks very much as it has done for many centuries past. The British Council recently selected Richmond as the typical English market town; but in its resistance of the sort of modern development to which other market towns have largely succumbed it has earned a better compliment than 'typical'. Unique, yes.

Richmond has long been associated with the military, a traditional connection greatly emphasised by a series of extensions to the nearby Catterick Camp, which has grown into one of the largest military establishments in England. Catterick Camp has become a town in itself, larger in area than Richmond: a vast complex of barracks and dwellings and administrative offices supplemented by many shopping arcades and religious and recreational facilities. But its ties, socially and economically, with the mother town, stay strong. Catterick is the garrison, Richmond the garrison town.

Richmond, with a population of around 7000, is the only town (begging Kirkby Stephen's pardon) visited on our route. It is too good to be by-passed.

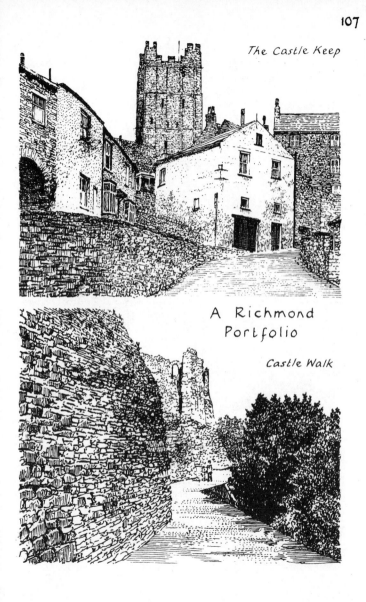

The Castle Keep

A Richmond
Portfolio

Castle Walk

Holy Trinity Church
Market Place

Waterfalls
on the Swale

Grey Friars' Tower

The Georgian Theatre

Dogs' Toilet
on the river bank

NOTE: Toilets
are also provided
in the town for
human ladies
and gentlemen

Richmond Bridge

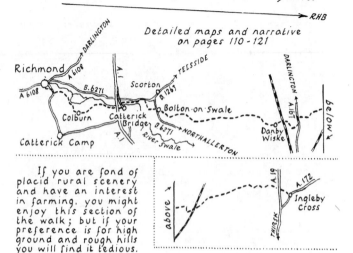

SECTION MAP : *RICHMOND to INGLEBY CROSS* : 23 miles

Detailed maps and narrative
on pages 110 - 121

If you are fond of placid rural scenery and have an interest in farming, you might enjoy this section of the walk; but if your preference is for high ground and rough hills you will find it tedious.

This crossing from Swaledale to the Cleveland Hills is the only section of the route that lies wholly over low ground. There is no escape to uncultivated heath or moorland even briefly.   On the Ordnance map 'hills' and 'moors' are plentiful but these place-names are misleading: note instead the contours, which nowhere rise even to a paltry 300 feet. Here is a twenty-mile gap, a fertile plain little above the sea: it is the northern extension of the Vale of York and known locally as the Vale of Mowbray — and there is no way of bridging it. Rich it is, in farming terms, much of it being arable with barley as the main crop, and quite unspoilt and indeed unvisited by tourists. According to the map almost the whole distance can be covered on footpaths and bridleways over which the public have the right to pass, but in practice one finds most of them so rarely used that they have virtually gone by default. The best way to cover these twenty miles of rural tranquillity is to get over them quickly by the use of country lanes and roads that are quiet and traffic-free, restricting field crossings on rights of way to the minimum necessary to maintain a reasonably direct course.

In the absence of accommodation along the route, it is advisable to aim to reach Ingleby Cross (inn) by nightfall, but at Oaktree Hill (16 miles) a bus route is reached that makes it possible to break the journey by a diversion to Northallerton (much accommodation) for the night.

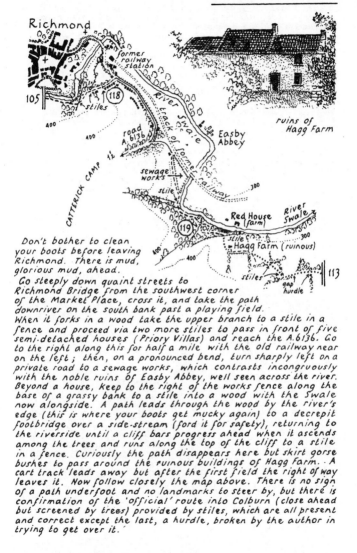

Richmond

former railway station

River Swale

track of former railway

road A.6136

CATTERICK CAMP 1½

sewage works

stile

Easby Abbey

ruins of Hagg Farm

Red House (farm)

River Swale

stile

Hagg Farm (ruinous)

stiles

gap hurdle

Don't bother to clean your boots before leaving Richmond. There is mud, glorious mud, ahead.

Go steeply down quaint streets to Richmond Bridge from the southwest corner of the Market Place, cross it, and take the path downriver on the south bank past a playing field. When it forks in a wood take the upper branch to a stile in a fence and proceed via two more stiles to pass in front of five semi-detached houses (Priory Villas) and reach the A.6136. Go to the right along this for half a mile with the old railway near on the left; then, on a pronounced bend, turn sharply left on a private road to a sewage works, which contrasts incongruously with the noble ruins of Easby Abbey, well seen across the river. Beyond a house, keep to the right of the works fence along the base of a grassy bank to a stile into a wood with the Swale now alongside. A path leads through the wood by the river's edge (this is where your boots get mucky again) to a decrepit footbridge over a side-stream (ford it for safety), returning to the riverside until a cliff bars progress ahead when it ascends among the trees and runs along the top of the cliff to a stile in a fence. Curiously the path disappears here but skirt gorse bushes to pass around the ruinous buildings of Hagg Farm. A cart track leads away but after the first field the right of way leaves it. Now follow closely the map above. There is no sign of a path underfoot and no landmarks to steer by, but there is confirmation of the 'official' route into Colburn (close ahead but screened by trees) provided by stiles, which are all present and correct except the last, a hurdle, broken by the author in trying to get over it.

The old village of Colburn (there is a large modern estate of houses nearby, but out of sight) is entered by the marshy side of a beck, too deep and wide to ford but avoided by a path on the left, which emerges into a lane at a stile: at its end cross the green via a bridge to the village street, which has an inn, the Hildyard Arms.

The bridleway onwards from Colburn no longer exists in its initial stages along the line shown on Ordnance maps owing to subsidence, but the farmer at the end of the street has kindly agreed to the crossing of his land by a cart-track to the point where the bridleway becomes tenable. Go to the right through the farmyard (which has some buildings with unusual features), turning left at the end through an iron gate. The cart-track goes straight ahead from this point: use it to cross two fields but in the third leave it to strike left to the far corner, where the bridleway is joined. It runs pleasantly east with the wooded banks of the Swale on the left. A continuous noise starts to assail the ears on this section: the sound of traffic on the A.1, a mile ahead. A fence is crossed (gate and stile) beyond which the bridleway becomes less distinct but trend slightly right to join the access road to St. Giles Farm at another stile, leaving it after 100 yards to follow a wire fence on the left along the top of the wooded bank of the Swale. Two long fields forward a fenced lane is entered to reach Thornbrough Farm. By this time the din of the A.1 has risen to crescendo, and suddenly there it is just ahead and unexpectedly below eye-level, crossing the Swale on a bridge with no architectural merit. Go steeply down to the river, pass under the bridge and then another carrying a disused railway and so emerge at the busy road junction of Catterick Bridge, on the site of CATARACTONIUM, a Roman town but dominated today by a modern race course.

Escape from the tumult here by crossing the bridge to its north end, where a stile on the right admits to the Swale, and continue pleasantly along the river bank, becoming accompanied by an ancient buttressed wall thought to be a Roman embankment. Beyond it a thin path goes forward around a curve of the river until obstructed by a gravel works. Enter this and turn left to continue on the road alongside (B.6271) to a fenced lane (a sign says TILCON); go along this, turning left on another fenced lane with Bolton-on-Swale Church straight ahead in trees.

Catterick Bridge

Colburn Hall, seen off route on the left, is an interesting rebuilt Tudor mansion with a separate Manor Hall nearby.

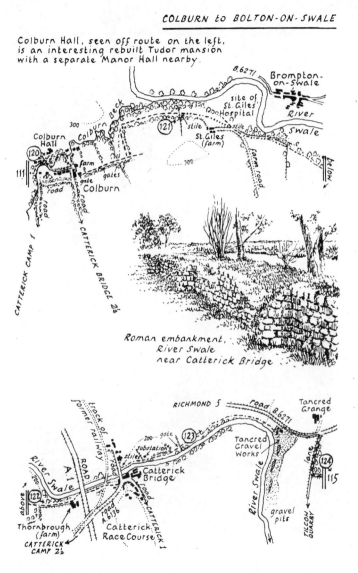

Roman embankment, River Swale near Catterick Bridge

The Jenkins Memorial,
St. Mary's Churchyard,
Bolton-on-Swale.

Believe it or not,
Henry Jenkins was born
at Ellerton-on-Swale in
the year 1500 and died
there in 1670 at the
age of 169.

This monument
was erected by public
contribution in 1743 to
commemorate his long
life: a well-deserved
recognition of
a remarkable
achievement.

St. Mary's Church,
Bolton-on-Swale

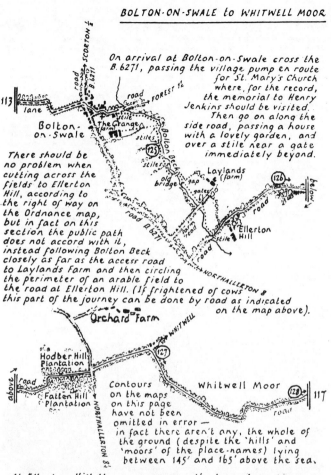

On arrival at Bolton-on-Swale cross the B.6271, passing the village pump en route for St. Mary's Church where, for the record, the memorial to Henry Jenkins should be visited. Then go on along the side road, passing a house with a lovely garden, and over a stile near a gate immediately beyond.

There should be no problem when cutting across the fields to Ellerton Hill, according to the right of way on the Ordnance map, but in fact on this section the public path does not accord with it, instead following Bolton Beck closely as far as the access road to Laylands Farm and then circling the perimeter of an arable field to the road at Ellerton Hill. (If frightened of cows this part of the journey can be done by road as indicated on the map above).

Contours on the maps on this page have not been omitted in error — in fact there aren't any, the whole of the ground (despite the 'hills' and 'moors' of the place-names) lying between 145' and 165' above the sea.

At Ellerton Hill there commences the longest continuous section of road-walking on the journey — eight miles of it to Oaktree Hill — not necessarily because we are afraid of cows but because the roads offer much the quickest means of progress on foot in a district where most other rights of way are suspect or at best wasteful of time. So off you go, on the grass verge, left right left right...

Top map amended 1994

To walkers whose liking is for high places and rough terrain, this will seem the dullest part of the whole walk; those who believe the earth is flat will be mightily encouraged on this section. The scenery is 100% rural, and all is tidily and pleasantly arranged, but views are restricted to the road and the fields adjoining: there is no distance to attract the eye, no stimulating prospect apart from the faraway outline of the Cleveland Hills, too remote yet to excite. You have heard of Yorkshire's broad acres: here they are in person, interminable, neatly patterned by clipped thorn hedges or wooden fences, but never, never, a stone wall: a foreign land indeed. Happily the road is almost traffic-free — you might

walk the full length without meeting a car until the A.167 is reached — and provided with ample grass verges that are kinder to the feet than the tarmac, but tedium grows apace and one plods onwards mechanically, head down, thinking nostagically of places left behind: Lakeland, limestone country, the Dales. Although in the midst of a thriving husbandry, few people are seen; in fact, one feels lonelier here than one does on the mountains. There is nothing to see, nothing worthy of illustration, nothing of interest to anyone but farmers. Walking as a pastime is unheard of and incomprehensible. There are no welcoming 'bed and breakfast' notices, no signs that say TEAS or even TEAZ. You feel out of place.

Danby Wiske, the only village, is less attractive than its name. You might, with luck, get a bag of crisps at the inn but certainly not a meal or a sandwich. You are tired and hungry but nobody wants to know. At 110 feet above the sea, Danby Wiske is the lowest point between the coastal extremities of the walk. Verily a slough of despond.

The author made attempts to vary the 8 miles of road-walking by resorting to rights of way shown on the Ordnance map, only to be beaten back to the tarmac by barbed wire, dykes, too-friendly bovines and other obstacles. It is better to stick to the road in this section and get on quickly.

Danby Wiske
Church

At Oaktree Hill there is an opportunity to catch a bus to Northallerton for the night, returning here by the morning bus: a course recommended if the calendar is of no consequence. Otherwise walk north along the A 167 for a quarter of a mile and escape into a grassy lane on the right, a sylvan paradise by contrast.

*It is reported that the inn now provides refreshments.

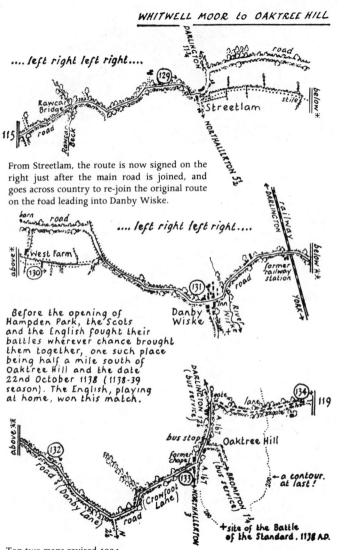

.... *left right left right*....

DARLINGTON 11¾

road

129

Rawcar Bridge

Rawcar Beck

115

road

Streetlam

stile

below *

NORTHALLERTON 5¼

From Streetlam, the route is now signed on the right just after the main road is joined, and goes across country to re-join the original route on the road leading into Danby Wiske.

barn road

.... *left right left right*....

railway

DARLINGTON

West Farm

above *

130

131

road

former railway station

Danby Wiske

Inn

River Wiske

YORK →

Before the opening of Hampden Park, the Scots and the English fought their battles wherever chance brought them together, one such place being half a mile south of Oaktree Hill and the date 22nd October 1138 (1138-39 season). The English, playing at home, won this match.

DARLINGTON 11½ (bus service)

gate

lane

134

119

bus stop

Oaktree Hill

former chapel

A 167

BROMPTON (bus service)

← a contour, at last!

above **

132

road (Danby Lane)

133

(Crowfoot Lane)

road

N

NORTHALLERTON 3

A 167

+ site of the Battle of the Standard. 1138 A.D.

Top two maps revised 1994

Harlsey Grove:
a moated farmstead

Rights of Way

A right of way is defined as "a right established by usage to pass over another's land."

Public roads are dedicated for the use of the public at large, on wheels or on foot, and are therefore rights of way unless prohibition is imposed on specified forms of progression (pedestrians on motorways, for example) by the highways authorities.

Private roads, including most farm access roads, have no rights of way unless such are established by use and recorded on the footpath maps maintained by the local authorities for the district.

Common ground may be freely wandered over by all.

What are more usually referred to as walkers' rights of way are *public footpaths* and *bridleways* over private land. Such rights may be legally provided in title deeds or they may simply have developed by the tread of feet over a period so long that "the memory of man runneth not to the contrary." Where rights of way do exist it is incumbent upon the owner or tenant to permit through access by means of stiles or gates and keep the route free from hazard. Where a public footpath is in general use these conditions are invariably observed, but where little or no use is made of rights of way by the public there is a natural tendency to disregard their existence and cease to maintain them. This happens frequently in the section from Richmond to Ingleby Cross, where the footpaths are not only invisible on the ground but often blocked by obstructions, including bulls.

The rights of way incorporated in this section of the route are not free from hazards at the time of writing, but the difficulties in negotiating them experienced by the author have been reported in gruesome detail to the North Riding County Council, who have kindly undertaken a survey, as the result of which a smoother passage can be expected by future travellers.

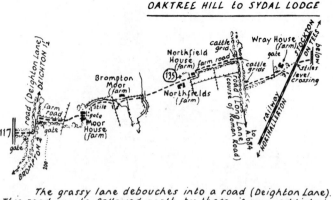

The grassy lane debouches into a road (Deighton Lane). This road can be followed north by those, if any, addicted to road-walking, taking a branch road east and so rejoining the direct route at the far end of Low Moor Lane. But the direct route as shown on these maps, following rights of way across country, is not only pleasanter but saves a mile in distance if nothing in time. The first part of this recommended short cut is, however, at the time of writing, difficult to negotiate between Moor House and Long Lane because of the absence of stiles and the presence of barbed wire, but probably by the time of publication a through route will have been established by the County Council.

From Long Lane to Low Moor Lane there is less difficulty, the right of way being recognised by stiles although not clear on the ground: the key is a single plank forming a bridge over Ing Beck.

At the far end of Low Moor Lane cross the West Rounton-East Harlsey road and enter, between imposing gateposts, the farm-road-cum-drive almost opposite: this is the approach to Sydal Lodge, ahead amid trees, and is also a right of way.

Map revised 1994.
*The barbed wire has now been removed, and stiles erected.

Brecken Hill

Ingleby
Arncliffe

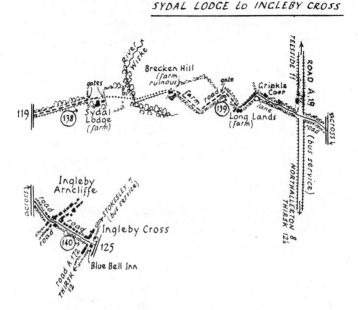

On the approach to Sydal Lodge the Cleveland Hills are seen
clearly ahead, the contraption on the skyline being a booster
television station, useful as a guide to the start of the long
tramp over the moors to the North Sea, positively the last
stage of the walk.

Sydal Lodge is almost hidden in fine trees. Pass alongside
farm buildings and straight on down a field to a footbridge
over the sluggish River Wiske (the same stream we saw at
Danby, being destined to meander aimlessly and hopelessly
around the countryside in a vain search for a contour that
would give it an objective). From the footbridge go up to
the derelict buildings of Brecken Hill, now a pig farm, and
here join an improving cart-track that winds along past the
farms of Long Lands and Crinkle Carr to reach the tumult of
the very busy double carriageway of the A.19 road. Crossing
this race-track is the last hazard of the day: summon up
the last vestiges of energy to scurry across at top speed
into the calm of a byroad leading to the pleasant village
of Ingleby Arncliffe (ice cream at the post office), whence
it continues downhill to the A.172 at Ingleby Cross.

If accommodation has been booked or is available at the
Blue Bell Inn, well and good; failing this there is a large
hotel, the Cleveland Tontine, one mile south on the A.172.

SECTION MAP : *INGLEBY CROSS TO CLAY BANK TOP* : 12¼ miles

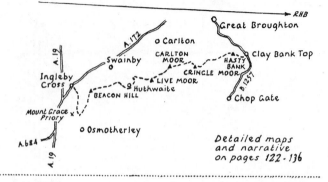

Detailed maps and narrative on pages 122-136

This is the finest section of our marathon (outside Lakeland) — a splendid high-level traverse along the escarpment of the Cleveland Hills: beautiful country with far-reaching views.

The path from Beacon Hill onwards is (thanks to Lyke Wake walkers) blazed almost as wide as a road, and, with signs at the few points of doubt, only a genius could go astray. The problem here is not route-finding but accommodation at the end of the day, a matter fully discussed on page 136, and it may well be advisable to ring ahead for a bed before leaving Ingleby Cross (or Huthwaite Green, where the last telephone is) having considered the weather, the hours of daylight and one's personal prowess, if any, as a resolute walker.

This is the start of the long crossing of the North York Moors and he will enjoy it most who has read about them in advance.

A few notes are appended but do not substitute for books written by others with a greater knowledge of the area. For 16 miles our route follows the line of the Lyke Wake Walk, including 12 that also coincide with the Cleveland Way, both of these long-distance pedestrian routes being the subjects of informed and interesting books.

For general reading the following publications are strongly recommended:

The Blue Bell Inn Ingleby Cross

NORTH YORK MOORS NATIONAL PARK (*H.M. Stationery Office*)
LYKE WAKE WALK by Bill Cowley
THE CLEVELAND WAY by Bill Cowley } (*Dalesman Publishing Co. Ltd*)

The North York Moors

The broad expanse of moorland extending for 30 miles from the Vale of Mowbray to the east coast, heatherclad, unenclosed, uninhabited, remote from industry and noise and free from traffic, is a magnificent territory for the walker: open country like the Pennines and the Cheviots yet more handsome and colourful — and friendlier by far. It is a wilderness crossed by few roads but many ancient tracks, a plateau high above the valleys yet of sleek and rounded slopes and easy gradients, where one can wander tirelessly all day and enjoy freedom complete; an elevated desert neither arid nor sterile but abounding in interest and beauty. And not only the walker will find a delight here. For the archaeologist, the searcher after objects ancient, the moors tell the story of the primitive people who settled here in ages past when climatic conditions for a time were kinder and the hills, then wooded, served both as home and hunting ground: their cairns and earthworks, barrows and burial mounds remain to this day remarkably profuse; of the Romans who flitted across the scene briefly leaving little of present interest excepting a road, recently partially restored, and signal stations; of Scandinavian invaders who, later, first set the patterns of community life that have survived; most of the village names have a Norse or Danish origin. The botanist and naturalist, the geologist and mineralogist, are all catered for on the wild hills and in the sheltered valleys. Today it is hard to believe that these uplands were formerly exploited for the wealth below the surface, but in fact they have been worked extensively for iron and coal, and, distinctively, for jet and alum. These industries are now all abandoned and nature is hiding their traces although the tracks of the mineral railways, the iron workings and jet spoilheaps are likely to be permanent reminders.   New industries of recent date are producing natural gas and potash while forestry operations are spreading along the hillsides; quite incongruous in an area remarkable for its prehistoric relics is an ultra-modern Ballistic Missile Early Warning Station.

The geographical boundaries of the area are clearly defined by a surround of valleys. To the north is Teesside; to the west is the Vale of Mowbray, to the south is the Vale of Pickering and the eastern boundary is the coastal strip: all lowlying land, and in their midst rises quite sharply the high plateau with its backbone on a west-east axis and of remarkably consistent altitude but indented by deep valleys, longer in the south where the slopes are gentler than they are northwards. Separating the valleys are high ridges. Each valley has its stream, feeding one of three main rivers: the Esk (north), the Rye and the Derwent (south).

The absence of walls and fences gives a rare feeling of freedom to expeditions 'over the tops' and two pedestrian routes recently inaugurated are proving very popular. One is the Lyke Wake Walk, an arduous 40-mile tramp having a time limit of 24 hours; the other is the 100-mile marathon known as the Cleveland Way. With both, as instigator of one and supporter of the other, the name of Bill Cowley is indelibly associated.

ANCIENT.......

The Church,
Mount Grace
Priory

Mount Grace Priory

Dating from 1398, Mount Grace Priory is one of the best surviving examples of the few Carthusian foundations in this country. The monks lived here in seclusion, almost as hermits, each isolated in his own cell with a garden, observing a rule of strict silence. The arrangement of the monks' quarters around a large walled cloister can be clearly seen. The central building within the grounds of the Priory was the Church, the tower being still intact. The ruins are open to the public and maintained by the Ministry of Public Buildings and Works. Adjoining is the former Priory Guest House, still partly in use.

.... AND MODERN

Television booster station
on Beacon Hill

From Ingleby Cross, take the side-road at the Blue Bell Inn signposted 'Arncliffe Hall and Church', passing both and also a farm beyond. When the road, now rough, turns sharp right enter a field-gate on the left and go up the field to another gate at the top, there meeting a forest road. Waste no time searching for a path straight up the steep wooded slopes (as indicated on Ordnance 2½" maps) — new forest roads have cut it to shreds and undergrowth has made a direct way to the top of Beacon Hill impassable. There is now no practicable alternative to following the forest road to the right for a full mile to the forest boundary, where turn sharp left (a sign says 'Moors Path') on a rising track through scrub to the top of the moor above the trees. Now, through a wicket-gate, continue with a fence on the left and a wall on the right, in heather and amongst regenerated birch, past a T.V. booster station of revolting appearance, until a break in the wall, much trodden, announces arrival at the Ordnance Survey column (numbered S.4413) on the east side. Cross over and touch it. It is famous. It marks the start of the Lyke Wake Walk and is a symbol of optimism.

Notice especially the attractive Arncliffe Hall, a Georgian house designed by John Carr of York (1754)

Arncliffe Church

Mount Grace Priory can be visited en route by a path from Park House — but if the day's sights are set beyond the B.1257 road at Hasty Bank there isn't time for this detour: save the Priory for a separate visit in the future.

Osmotherley has a large Youth Hostel with rooms for non-members

Map amended 1994.

The Ordnance column on Beacon Hill, looking north-east

looking north-east across Scarth Nick.
The path to Scugdale is indicated (-~-~-).

Beacon Hill

Beacon Hill, although less than a thousand feet above sea level, is a splendid viewpoint, the panorama being greatly enhanced by its abrupt rise from the plains, the hill forming an upthrust cornerstone. Southwards, stretching apparently to the bounds of the earth, is the Vale of York; westwards is the long line of the Pennines beyond the Vale of Mowbray, a conspicuous indentation indicating Swaledale; northwards the hills of Durham are seen across the Cleveland Plain and Teesside — a wide prospect indeed, and, standing here, one can readily appreciate the importance of this signalling station long ago. It is to the east, however, that attention should be focussed, for in this direction is the line our march follows: the scene is a wilderness of heather moors sharply terminated by the pronounced Cleveland escarpment. It promises well.

From the Ordnance column keep to the well-blazed path by the wall, north-east, as far as a gate (with notice affixed: details below), from which it heads across the open moor as a wide scar in the heather, declining gently at first and then, when the wall again comes alongside, steeply to the tarmac road in Scarth Nick. Across the road, just above a cattle grid and in the midst of sundry notices (LWW means Lyke Wake Walk), a wicket-gate admits to a plantation and a narrow, bumpy path, which soon improves. At a prominent spoil-heap on the left there commences a steep descent into the pleasant valley of Scugdale, turning right at a 'Moors Path' sign upon reaching a gated lane to Swainby and continuing thence up the valley on a distinct path.

Notice affixed to a gate on Beacon Hill:

BE YE MAN OR BE YE WOMAN
BE YE GOING OR BE YE COMIN'
BE YE SOON OR BE YE LATE
BE YE SURE TO SHUT THIS GATE
RIPON C.S. SCHOOL
21st JUNE 1968

*Cleveland Way sign

Scugdale, from Coalmire

The path to
Live Moor is
indicated
(- - - -)

Carlton Moor

Live Moor

*Cairn on tumulus,
summit of Live Moor*

Carlton Moor

Live Moor

SCUGDALE to HOLEY MOOR

The path up Scugdale is as wide and well-defined as a gravel footway in an urban public park, and, being rural, is even more pleasant, the valley being wooded, with many fine deciduous trees alongside the beck and new coniferous plantations on the higher slopes. After three-quarters of a mile, a motley assembly of signposts heralds a wicket-gate on the left and leaves the traveller in no doubt that it should be used. The field thus entered slopes down to another gate giving access to a ford on a tributary of Scugdale Beck. Across this, a road is joined at a bridge over the main stream and followed up to a junction with the main valley-road. Here, to the right

of a telephone kiosk, a path goes up the facing hillside, passing a disused iron mine and reaching a signboard (Bridle road to Faceby) where turn left, keeping below a plantation until a break in the latter is reached. Urged on by another flurry of signs, ascend this break: it is both steep and slippery. At the top is the open moor. There is no mistaking the path, which climbs very clearly onto the plateau of Live Moor, and is plainly visible beyond on the long slope of Carlton Moor. The route is now straightforward and foolproof, needing neither direction signs nor directions. Just keep plodding ahead.

The ford in Scugdale

Scugdale is one of the many Cleveland valleys mined for jet and the spoil heaps of the disused workings can be seen along the 900' contour, looking like a series of giant molehills.

*'motley assembly of signposts' no longer there

Boundary stone and Ordnance column,
summit of Carlton Moor

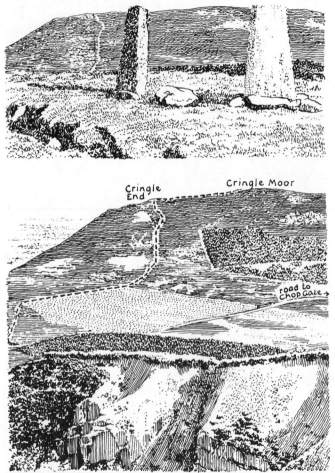

Cringle
End

Cringle Moor

road to
Chop Gate →

Cringle Moor, from the old alum workings on Carlton Moor.
The path to Cringle Moor is indicated (-----).

Along the gentle rise to **Carlton Moor** is a line of white-topped boundary stones, one of them plumb in the middle of the broad path. As the top is breasted a great surprise awaits walkers who have not done their homework by reading up the route in advance. For half a mile the landscape is eerily lunar, the heather having been stripped off and the surface bulldozed and levelled to make runways for a gliding club whose buildings can be seen ahead. In due course this arid desert will be grassed and pleasanter to walk upon: in the meantime prefer a path along the edge of the rising escarpment to the Ordnance Survey column (No. S 4421) on the top of Carlton Moor, noting below the conspicuous pink spoilheaps of the old jet workings strung along the hillside. This is a bold viewpoint with an uninterrupted prospect forward to the next height on the route, Cringle Moor; more to the north the sharp peak of Roseberry Topping (accentuated by quarrying into a miniature Matterhorn) is conspicuous and the monument to Captain Cook on Easby Moor can be distinguished. A motor road runs through the depression ahead (Carlton Bank); descend to it, roughly, along the edge of a crater (a disused alum mine) that has radically changed the natural contours of the ground. Cross the road and take any one of three paths to the flat moor beyond: they all converge to skirt a fenced field and ascend, with a wall on the left, to the stony promontory of Cringle End, another fine viewpoint.

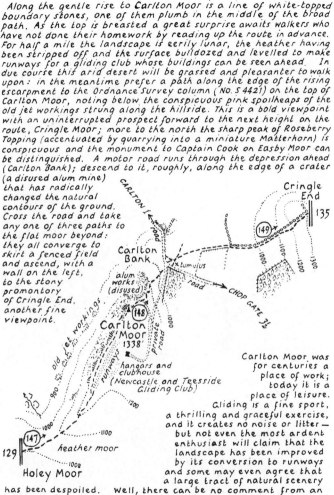

Carlton Moor was for centuries a place of work; today it is a place of leisure. Gliding is a fine sport, a thrilling and graceful exercise, and it creates no noise or litter — but not even the most ardent enthusiast will claim that the landscape has been improved by its conversion to runways and some may even agree that a large tract of natural scenery has been despoiled. Well, there can be no comment from an 'off-comer', except to say that if such an operation was to be planned for the top of Helvellyn all hell would be let loose.

Boundary stone, view indicator and seat,
Cringle End

Cold Moor, from Cringle Moor

The path to Cold Moor
is indicated (-----)

Cairn on tumulus,
summit of Cringle Moor

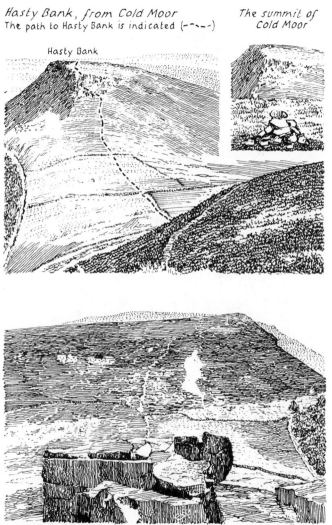

Hasty Bank, from Cold Moor
The path to Hasty Bank is indicated (-·-·-)

The summit of Cold Moor

Hasty Bank

looking back to Cold Moor (overtopped by Cringle Moor), from the top of the Wainstones.

The Wainstones:
the lower rocks

The Wainstones:
the upper rocks

looking across Clay Bank Top from Hasty Bank

The path to Urra Moor
is indicated (‑‑‑‑‑)

Clay Bank Top

car park

  Cringle Moor is the finest elevation so far reached along the escarpment, being not only the second highest summit on the Cleveland hills but having a steep and craggy declivity falling from its northern rim. The path turns up along the edge of the downfall, not visiting the actual summit of the moor, which is crowned with a tumulus and a cairn, and then goes down to a depression, with walled enclosures, beyond which it ascends to the top of Cold Moor, an airy dome carpeted with heather and bilberry. History then repeats itself, Cold Moor being descended to a similar depression with walled enclosures beyond which is another rise. But this one is different, being decorated with a cluster of fanged and pinnacled rocks, the Wainstones: a popular rock-climbing ground. Other groups of large boulders are nearby. There are natural shelters here from rain and wind (and sun!). This is an enjoyable section, a change from heather, and there is no difficulty in scrambling between the buttresses to the easy ground above.
You will like the Wainstones.

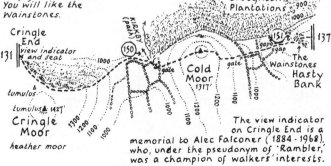

Cringle
End
view indicator
and seat
131

tumulus

tumulus 1427'

Cringle
Moor

heather moor

KIRKBY
(path)
150
1000

Broughton
Plantations

Cold
Moor
1317

gate

151
gap
gap
137

The
Wainstones
Hasty
Bank

The view indicator on Cringle End is a memorial to Alec Falconer (1884-1968), who, under the pseudonym of 'Rambler,' was a champion of walkers' interests.

At Clay Bank Top.......

Clay Bank Top, where the road B1257 from Bilsdale crosses a natural (but artificially afforested) pass through the hills and starts its descent to the Cleveland Plain, is obviously a place for taking stock.

Most walkers on arrival here from Ingleby Cross will be feeling the effect of 12 up and down miles and be ready to call it a day. But where can a bed be found? There are no habitations near and they must be sought, but north or south? Happily the Helmsley - Middlesbrough bus service comes through here and can be used by those whose arrival at the road coincides with the bus timetable, although this is unlikely to happen unless planned, there being only two or three buses a day (at the time of writing). Failing this, a hitch may be begged. (The nearest telephone-box, if a taxi can be afforded, is inconvenient.) Or, dammit, you can walk — it's downhill. Go north, young man. Northwards is Great Broughton (2½ miles) and Stokesley (5 miles), both having accommodation and the advantage of a morning bus back to Clay Bank Top where the journey can be resumed. Bilsdale, south, can be ruled out: the nearest communities (2½ miles) are Seave Green and Chop Gate, not at all tourist conscious, and not unlikely to suspect, if you ask for a bed, that you are suggesting a sexual adventure, which, of course, is ridiculous, (or is it?)

Only strong walkers should consider proceeding further on the route today. Beyond the B1257 there is but one habitation before Glaisdale, and this solitary building, the Lion Inn at Blakey, has no accommodation to offer (at present, 1971; but some is planned). The Lion is 10 miles distant and it could be reached in 3 hours, the walking being remarkably easy. If necessary, the telephone there can be used to hire a taxi to take you to a bed. Youth hostellers on this section will be aiming for the Westerdale hostel — an even longer trek.

In a situation like this the man who carries his bed and breakfast on his back has the last laugh.

....

SECTION MAP : *CLAY BANK TOP to GLAISDALE :* 18¾ *miles*

Detailed maps and narrative on pages 136-149

....

Hasty Bank is even better than Cringle Moor, the Wainstones being succeeded by a fine traverse along its edge and exciting glimpses down a fringe of steep crags; ahead, across a profound gap, is seen the next stage of the walk over Urra Moor. The path leads roughly down a bracken slope with spoilheaps to a stile at the junction of a forest fence and a stone wall, beyond which is another stile and a flight of steps down to a tarmac road, the important B.1257 linking Helmsley and Stokesley.

<----- Here consult the notes opposite

The route crosses the road to a gate directly opposite: this is Hagg's Gate. Go through it (signs are profuse again) and up by the wall serving as a forest boundary. For the first time since leaving Beacon Hill the path is not distinct on the ground here, the boots of thousands of walkers having caused little impression on the grass, but above a stile in a fence it becomes clear again as it wriggles up a cleft in a rock outcrop to reach easier slopes above. Note the ancient dykes on the right, the original purpose of which is obscure. Also the stunted larches over the wall on the left, the last trees that will be seen at close quarters for the next 17 miles.

The path goes on as straight as an arrow along the level peaty crest of Carr Ridge.

Hasty Bank is the most impressive of the Cleveland hills and its fine summit deserves a distinctive name of its own, Hasty Bank properly being the southern slope of the hill above a farmhouse of that name. It deserves a cairn, too.

looking back from the firebreak on Urra Moor

Cringle Moor   Cold Moor   Hasty Bank

cairn on tumulus,
Urra Moor

Ordnance column on tumulus,
summit of Urra Moor

The actual top is Round Hill
(a reference to the tumulus),
usually named Botton Head.

URRA MOOR to BLOWORTH

The Hand Stone and the old road,
Urra Moor

The path along Carr Ridge starts to rise gently to Urra Moor.
The surroundings are featureless, but it is interesting to see,
eastwards on the hillside across the hollow of Ingleby Botton, a
distinct scar indicating the incline of the old Rosedale railway,
with which we shall soon be on intimate terms. The path reaches
a firebreak (ground stripped of heather to prevent fires spreading)
at a notice-board, and here slants up left along it as wide as a road
(which it originally was), passing a tumulus (cairned) on the right. A
white Ordnance column on the left (No. 2988), also on a tumulus,
marks the highest point on the Cleveland hills. On the 'roadside'
nearby is the Hand Stone, and other inscribed stones are
met as the highway, with its original paving visible in
places, descends gradually to the old railway.

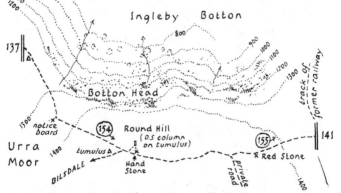

The Rosedale Ironstone Railway

The Rosedale Branch was constructed in 1861, when the North Eastern Railway extended its lines in Cleveland by incorporating a mineral line, replacing it by a single standard-gauge track and continuing it by means of a mile-long incline across the high moors at an elevation of around 1300' for ten miles to the ironstone mines in Rosedale — a considerable engineering achievement, the contours being so closely followed that, throughout a long passage across several watersheds, cuttings, embankments and levelling sufficed to carry the line around the heads of intervening valleys without the use of any bridges or tunnels. The track was unenclosed by fences and had no signalling equipment, operation being controlled by staff based on Blakey Ridge. This remarkable enterprise was undertaken to convey the high-grade iron ore mined on the Rosedale hillsides, which had in fact been worked from a very early date, possibly for two thousand years, as evidenced by ancient furnaces, and was enjoying a booming prosperity in the middle of last century. Road transport via Pickering was inadequate to cope with the output; the construction of a high-level railway over the moors, linking with other lines that served the big blast furnaces of Teesside and Durham, was a bold venture, and, despite storms and blizzards, appears to have well succeeded, upwards of ten million tons of iron ore being conveyed along it. Only freight trains used the line but occasionally a few passengers were carried.

The railway as originally laid entered Rosedale by way of Blakey Ridge and terminated at the Bank Top mines on the west side of the valley, where the main workings were located and which today can be identified by a prominent chimney,* one of the many relics still to be seen. In 1865 it was extended by a branch running around the head of the valley to mines on the eastern flank from the staff control point at Blakey, which then became a junction.

By the turn of the century ironstone production was in decline and the railway less in demand, and finally it was closed and dismantled in 1929. The line was lonely and isolated, and threatened by extreme weather conditions, but the regular passage of freight trains brought a pulse of life to the wilderness through which they passed. Today the track is still there, but it is silent; yet even in death it has lost nothing of its grace and dignity but remains a mute and inspiring monument to the men who planned and built it over a century ago, a permanent way that will remain permanent, a reminder of an achievement that deserves to be, and will be, long remembered.

A map of the railway is given overleaf ⟶

A fascinating description of the Rosedale mines and railway is found in a booklet, A HISTORY OF ROSEDALE by R.H.Hayes (25p) obtainable locally or from the Ryedale Folk Museum, Hutton le Hole, near Pickering.

*Chimney demolished 1972

BLOWORTH to DALE HEAD, FARNDALE

Bloworth Crossing

The railway track is joined at a 'Moors Path' sign. The Cleveland Way now turns off to the north and will not be met again until it is rejoined on the sea-cliffs at Hawsker Bottoms. Our own route still coincides with the Lyke Wake Walk, going to the right along the cinders of the permanent way. Two gates across it are passed; at the second the track is crossed by a rough moorland road. This is Bloworth Crossing; at this point there is a glimpse of Bransdale to the south. Keep on along the railway track, responding to the easy walking by a noticeable increase in speed. Beyond a cutting Farndale is in view and the track loops around the head of this valley on an even contour, keeping slightly below the watershed. No question of short-cutting the loops arises: one look at the terrain flanking the permanent way is enough to rule it out as a possibility. With little of interest to see, you might as well be improving your knowledge by reading the story of the railway as you go along. Don't worry, you won't fall into any holes.

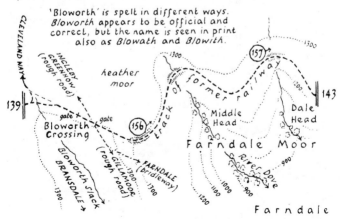

'Bloworth' is spelt in different ways. Bloworth appears to be official and correct, but the name is seen in print also as Blowath and Blowith.

The Rosedale Ironstone Railway
MAP

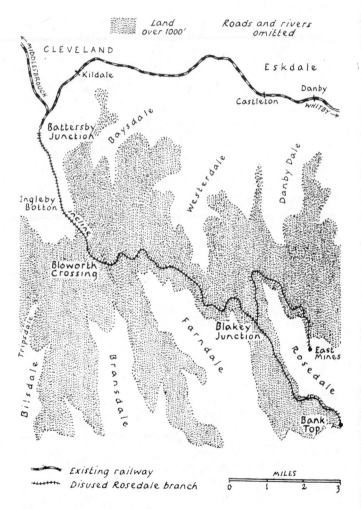

Land over 1000'

Roads and rivers omitted

CLEVELAND

MIDDLESBROUGH

Kildale

Eskdale

Danby

Castleton

WHITBY

Battersby Junction

Baysdale

Westerdale

Danby Dale

Ingleby Botton

Incline

Bloworth Crossing

Tripsdale

Bilsdale

Bransdale

Farndale

Blakey Junction

Rosedale

East Mines

Bank Top

Existing railway
Disused Rosedale branch

MILES
0   1   2   3

The long embankment near Esklets

Fast walking continues along the railway track and speeds will now have accelerated to 5 m.p.h.

Lyke Wake walkers depart left when a sign tells them to, bound for Esklets (a farmhouse seen half a mile away). Their route will again be met, briefly, at Rosedale Head. ✻

Youth hostellers bound for Westerdale should also turn off here, rejoining our route next morning at Rosedale Head.

The rest of us will resist the attractions of lovely Farndale ✻✻
(which specialises in daffodils, not beds) and surge on happily along the permanent way. We're enjoying this: it's like playing at trains again. Better than that, it's like being a train yourself.

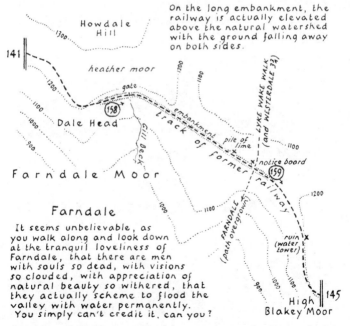

On the long embankment, the railway is actually elevated above the natural watershed with the ground falling away on both sides.

Howdale Hill
1300
141
heather moor
1200
gate
158
Dale Head
1100
1000
900
embankment
track of former railway
pile of lime
LYKE WAKE WALK (and WESTERDALE 3½)
notice board
159
1200
1100

Farndale Moor

Farndale

It seems unbelievable, as you walk along and look down at the tranquil loveliness of Farndale, that there are men with souls so dead, with visions so clouded, with appreciation of natural beauty so withered, that they actually scheme to flood the valley with water permanently.
You simply can't credit it, can you?

FARNDALE (path overgrown)
1000
1100
ruin (water tower)
900
1000
1100
High 145
Blakey Moor

*The Lyke Wake Walk now follows the same route as the Coast to Coast Walk, to the Lion Inn at Blakey. The Westerdale Youth Hostel is now closed.
**Accommodation is now available in Farndale.

A good moment. At a curve in the last railway cutting the Lion Inn comes into view on the skyline ahead.

The Lion Inn is the most obvious halting-place on the whole route: the first habitation since Huthwaite, 16 miles back. It may or may not have accommodation (if depending on it ring through to find out before starting the day's walk.) If starting from Clay Bank Top this is of less importance, the miles continuing very easy to Glaisdale. If marooned here it may be possible to get a lift to Castleton, or a taxi may be hired from there, returning you to the Lion next morning Or there is a ruin across the road where a miserable night could be spent.

The Lion Inn,
Blakey

Dating from 1553, the Lion is a bleak and isolated moorland inn. Situated amongst decayed relics of industry, its patrons are no longer ironworkers and coalminers; today it is a port of call for motorists and walkers.

Blakey Howe

Behind the inn is Blakey Howe, a tumulus excavated to provide a sheltered and secluded hollow for cockfighting, hence its alternative name of Cockpit Hill.

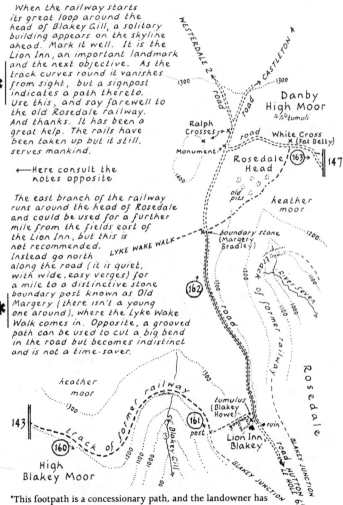

When the railway starts its great loop around the head of Blakey Gill, a solitary building appears on the skyline ahead. Mark it well. It is the Lion Inn, an important landmark and the next objective. As the track curves round it vanishes from sight, but a signpost indicates a path thereto. Use this, and say farewell to the old Rosedale railway. And thanks. It has been a great help. The rails have been taken up but it still. serves mankind.

* ←—— Here consult the notes opposite

The east branch of the railway runs around the head of Rosedale and could be used for a further mile from the fields east of the Lion Inn, but this is not recommended. Instead go north along the road (it is quiet, with wide, easy verges) for a mile to a distinctive stone boundary post known as Old Margery (there isn't a young one around), where the Lyke Wake Walk comes in. Opposite, a grooved path can be used to cut a big bend in the road but becomes indistinct and is not a time-saver.

**

WESTERDALE 2

CASTLETON 4

1300   1300

Danby High Moor

⁂ tumuli

Ralph Crosses ✕

road

White Cross ✕ (Fat Betty)

Monument ✕

163   →147

Rosedale Head

1400

old pits

heather moor

1200

boundary stone (Margery Bradley)

LYKE WAKE WALK

162

1300

track of former railway

River Seven

1100

1000

1200

road

Rosedale

heather moor

1300

track of former railway

1300

1200

1100

1000

tumulus (Blakey Howe)

143

160

High Blakey Moor

Blakey Gill

161

post ✕

ruin

Lion Inn Blakey

BLAKEY JUNCTION

BLAKEY JUNCTION

road

HUTTON LE HOLE 6½

*This footpath is a concessionary path, and the landowner has requested that all dogs should be kept under close control.

** The Lyke Wake Walk and the Coast to Coast Walk now march together to the Lion Inn at Blakey (*see new note on page 143*).

Monuments
at Rosedale Head

top left:
   Ralph Cross
      (Young Ralph)
top middle:
   White Cross
      (Fat Betty)
top right:
   Ralph Cross
      (Old Ralph)

Frank Elgee Memorial

A curve in the Rosedale road can be by-passed along a path following a series of white boundary stones and the corner of the Fryup cart-track may also be by-passed, but both short-cuts are often revoltingly slimy and it is then better to keep to the tarmac. At the Fryup turn (signpost: 'unsuitable for motors') the Lyke Wake Walk is departed from and not met again. The wide and gravelly Fryup track gives excellent walking and views of Eskdale with the sharp peak of Roseberry Topping conspicuous ten miles northwest, but after half a mile is forsaken in favour of a branch to the right leading to the solitary building now in sight. This is Trough House, a shooting box, roughly furnished and such an excellent refuge that one almost wishes it would rain cats and dogs so that advantage could be taken of its shelter. Beyond, the track deteriorates in an area of old coal pits and is overgrown with heather and bracken and rushes, although its course is plain to see rounding the head of Great Fryup Dale — of which there is a full-length view — and is accompanied by a thin path, which after ascending slightly finally heads straight for Glaisdale and joins a tarmac road. The ground now forms a ridge between Great Fryup Dale (left) and Glaisdale Head (right) and the road runs along its crest. Follow it north.

Danby High Moor is typical of this wedge of high country: now uninhabited and inhospitable but yielding evidence by the excavation of its many barrows or burial mounds of a primitive people who lived here three or four thousand years ago.

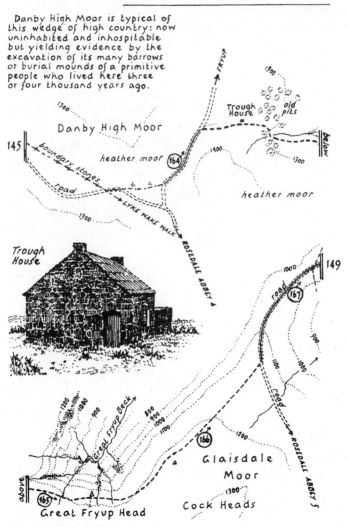

Top map amended 1994

Beggar's Bridge

After passing a fine cairn, 100 yards away on the right, the road turns slightly left near a white Ordnance Survey column. Leave it at this point and take the cart track going straight ahead: a sign declares this to be unsuitable for motors, but for foot-travellers it is a way par excellence heading directly down the declining ridge (Glaisdale Rigg), towards the end of which, with a wall close ahead, the track bears to the left (ignore all others) and descends alongside a fence, acquiring a tarmac surface beyond a gate and passing a covered reservoir to reach civilisation in the form of a modern housing estate at the top end of the village of Glaisdale. Turn right, and if in search of lodging or refreshment go down by the long terrace, where sundry delicacies including raw sausages may be acquired in exchange for money and where there are possibilities of obtaining accommodation. The route follows the road round to the railway station and the River Esk. The scenery in the vicinity of the river is charming. Pass under the railway bridge to take a photograph of the early-17th century Beggar's Bridge, as everyone does, then return under the railway and immediately take the path, steep initially, over a footbridge into East Arncliffe Wood. The path is overgrown but easy to follow, the middle section being roughly paved with stone slabs.

railway station

disused loading bays

road

road

Beggar's Bridge

River Esk

cart track

footbridge

ENVIRONS OF BEGGAR'S BRIDGE

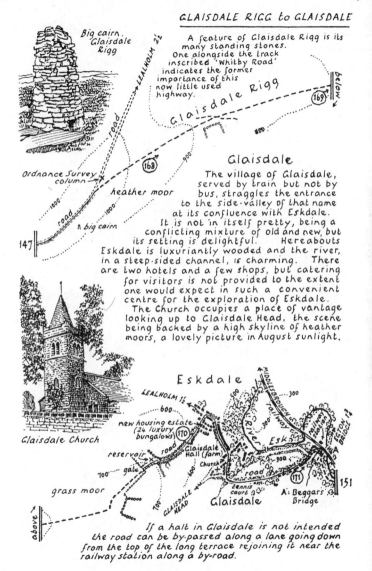

Big cairn
Glaisdale
Rigg

A feature of Glaisdale Rigg is its
many standing stones.
One alongside the track
inscribed 'Whitby Road'
indicates the former
importance of this
now little used
highway.

LEALHOLM 2¼

Glaisdale Rigg

169

below

800

Ordnance Survey
column

168

900

1800

heather moor

road

1000

147

A big cairn

Glaisdale

The village of Glaisdale,
served by train but not by
bus, straggles the entrance
to the side-valley of that name
at its confluence with Eskdale.
It is not in itself pretty, being a
conflicting mixture of old and new, but
its setting is delightful.   Hereabouts
Eskdale is luxuriantly wooded and the river,
in a steep-sided channel, is charming.   There
are two hotels and a few shops, but catering
for visitors is not provided to the extent
one would expect in such a convenient
centre for the exploration of Eskdale.
The Church occupies a place of vantage
looking up to Glaisdale Head, the scene
being backed by a high skyline of heather
moors, a lovely picture in August sunlight.

Glaisdale Church

Eskdale

MIDDLESBROUGH

LEALHOLM 1½

600

300

new housing estate
(24 luxury
bungalows)

170

Esk

railway

EGTON BRIDGE 1¾

reservoir

road

Glaisdale
Hall (farm)

river

300

gate

Church

700

road

171

151

grass moor

700

GLAISDALE HEAD

400

tennis
court

Glaisdale

A: Beggar's
Bridge

above

If a halt in Glaisdale is not intended
the road can be by-passed along a lane going down
from the top of the long terrace rejoining it near the
railway station along a by-road.

150

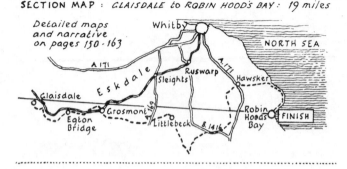

*Detailed maps
and narrative
on pages 150-163*

This final stage of the walk has a wide variety of scene:
a lovely river and woodlands, heather moors, charming
villages, prehistoric relics, a stately waterfall, a forest
trail, steam locomotives, and, to end it, an exhilarating
cliff path and the North Sea extending to a far horizon,
all different subjects alike only in distinctive appeal. In
fact many walkers will consider this section the best of
all, quite apart from the satisfaction of accomplishing a
mission. The 'going' for the greater part of it is easy and
a strong walker could reach Robin Hood's Bay from Claisdale
before nightfall, but country like this is much too good to
be hurried over, much too interesting to be appreciated in
full measure if limbs are tired, and it is suggested that the
day's activity be halted at Hawsker (the first opportunity
of a bed after Grosmont), leaving the last few miles to the
Bay — a splendid finish along the cliffs — until next day.

It will be noticed that, towards the end of the journey, the
shortest route to the Bay is not taken, five miles being added
by a wide detour to the north around Hawsker. This detour
can, of course, be omitted and the Bay reached more directly
by road, in which event an overnight stay en route will not
normally be necessary. The reason for the detour is simply
to give a fitting culmination to the walk, a counterpart to
the start over St. Bees Head, reaching Robin Hood's Bay over
the top of the sea-cliffs, by far the finest approach. It is
a little odd that this *west-to-east* walk started *north-west*
and ends *south-west*, but that's the way the best land lies.

You will really enjoy this last section to the Bay, whatever
the condition of your blisters, so much that you will regret
leaving behind each of its many attractive features. And
when the North Sea comes into full view and you recall your
last sighting of the Irish Sea you will be glad you didn't stay
on in Patterdale. Lakeland is all very well but by resisting
its lure you have seen so much new and interesting and lovely
country that, on reflection, you wouldn't have missed for worlds.
Come on now, admit it.

Egton Bridge

Egton is a village on the hillside a mile north of the Esk. The more sequestered Egton Bridge is the part of the parish built on the river banks and served by the railway. Here, as everywhere in the middle reaches of Eskdale, the scenery is delightful, a wealth of trees bordering the river and a belt of rich pastures, broken by extensive woodlands, descending to the valley from a surround of wild moors. Only the iron bridge offends the eye: it is quite out of character. There are some houses of distinction and two hotels of attractive design, but the building most worth a visit is the Roman Catholic church, which has coloured bas-relief panels on its exterior walls and ornate decoration internally on the ribbed roof. In such a sylvan setting little awareness is felt of the enclosing moors, desolate and inhospitable but revealing much of archaeological interest, mainly of prehistoric origin but with evidences of the Roman occupation of the area.

R.C. Church,
Egton Bridge

The path through East Arncliff Wood emerges on a quiet tarmac road (the moor road to Rosedale). Go down this to the left and so reach Egton Bridge, in lovely wooded surroundings: note the noble sequoias bordering the road. The bridge is a disappointment but take a look at the Roman Catholic Church, which isn't. Then, without fear of being turned back, enter upon the private estate-road of Egton Manor, armed with the knowledge that it is a public footpath and bridleway and no longer subject to tolls.

PLEASE do NOT enter the private driveway to Egton Manor.

149

EGTON 2

300....

railway station

200....

R.C.Church

GLAISDALE 2 (road)

173

railway

Egton Manor

private road

153

River ESK

Egton Bridge

200....

East Arncliff Wood

172

River ESK

KEEN

ROSEDALE ABBEY 7

300....

'Arncliff' is the Ordnance spelling; locally, 'Arncliff' or 'Arncliffe' is preferred.

Grosmont

At Grosmont a traveller down the valley of the Esk first becomes aware, albeit slightly, of urban influences. Here are the steep declivities to the river, the rich woodlands that so characterise the higher reaches, but the railway station (a junction of lines), the debris of iron workings, and a faint air of commercialism suggest that the best of the scenery is being left behind. Nevertheless it is an excellent centre for touring the district: there are shops and some accommodation is provided. A priory existed here at one time; today the religious needs of the Anglican community are served by a church set back from the houses in a hanging garden of trees by the river. Road access to the village is very steep on all sides, which would appear to explain the absence of a bus service: the railway here, a scenic joy, is still important.

The North York Moors
Railway Society

Steam locomotives
standing in
Grosmont Station

The railway
from Whitby to
Pickering, leaving
the Eskdale line at
Grosmont, threaded a
tortuous course through scenery
of rare beauty, and popular opinion
considered it one of the finest railways
in the country. It was one of George Stephenson's
early creations. Alas, like so many others, its day is done
and a notable engineering achievement would have become
yet another historical relic but for the valiant efforts of a
band of enthusiasts, the North York Moors Railway Society, to
preserve and continue to operate privately the section from
Grosmont to Goathland with steam locomotives and rolling
stock they have acquired. George Stephenson would approve.

Bridge over the Esk at Grosmont

The estate road passes a farm and then the former Toll Bar, which although no longer functional as such still displays details of the tolls formerly charged, these being made for the passage both of the living and the dead (Hearse...6d), before emerging on the Egton-Grosmont road, which follow to the right over a bridge (this is farewell to the River Esk) and past playing fields to the village of Grosmont, where reprieved steam locomotives may be on view at the railway station. Go over the level crossing and up the steep road beyond (1 in 3), ignoring two branches to Whitby on the left. As height is gained a fine retrospective view of Eskdale opens up.

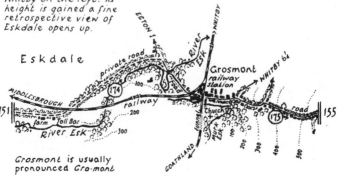

Grosmont is usually pronounced Gro-mont

*After stepping gingerly across a cattle grid the open moor is reached. The stones of the High Bride Stones that remain standing can be seen from the road. Just after passing a car park, turn left at a 'public footpath' sign to cross the moor. On reaching the busy Whitby–Pickering road, turn left and then turn right at a 'public bridleway' sign.

The Old Mill, Littlebeck

After stepping gingerly across a cattle grid the open moor is reached. A deviation to the right leads to Low Bride Stones, almost hidden in a swamp of rushes, and then, taking a course parallel to the road, to the more impressive High Bride Stones, some standing, some fallen. Now, in pathless heather, due east, cut across the road past the tumulus of Flat Howe to the busy Whitby-Pickering road, reaching it at a signpost pointing to Littlebeck (unsuitable for motors). The rough track indicated crosses open ground, enters a lane and is then joined by a road from Sleights for the steep descent to the hamlet of Littlebeck, a miniature Arcadia embowered in trees, a glimpse of heaven for nerve-frayed towndwellers. Across the beck and round the corner, near a seat below the house on the right, is the signposted start of the path to Falling Foss. Use this: it is easy to follow, but two branches to the left early on, in an area of old spoilheaps, are misleading. Thereafter the way is clear up the valley, always amongst trees, and finally rising gently to a massive boulder out of which, amazingly, has been carved a splendid shelter with seats: in beautiful lettering the name 'The Hermitage,' the year 1790 and the initials G.C. are inscribed in the stone. Here the Falling Foss Forest Trail is joined. Take the upper of two paths, rising towards the farm buildings of Newton House.

**The 'golf balls' were dismantled at the end of 1993, being replaced by a large pyramid.

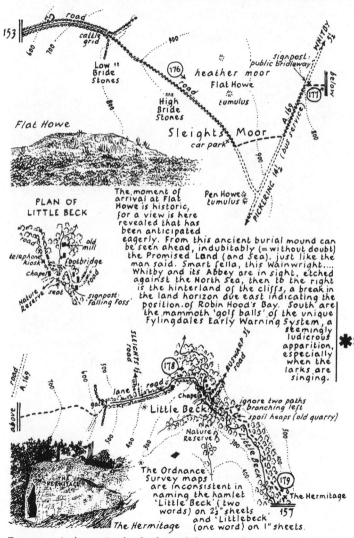

153

road

cattle grid

600 700

Low "Bride Stones

176

road

800

High Bride Stones

Flat Howe

Sleights Moor

car park

900

heather moor
Flat Howe

tumulus

signpost:
'public bridleway'

WHITBY 5½

moor below

171

A.169 (bus service)

PICKERING 14½

Pen Howe
tumulus

The moment of arrival at Flat Howe is historic, for a view is here revealed that has been anticipated eagerly. From this ancient burial mound can be seen ahead, indubitably (= without doubt) the Promised Land (and Sea), just like the man said. Smart fella, this Wainwright.... Whitby and its Abbey are in sight, etched against the North Sea, then to the right is the hinterland of the cliffs, a break in the land horizon due east indicating the position of Robin Hood's Bay. South are the mammoth 'golf balls' of the unique Fylingdales Early Warning System, a seemingly ludicrous apparition, especially when the larks are singing. **

PLAN OF LITTLE BECK

road

telephone kiosk

old mill

footbridge

chapel

road

Nature Reserve   seat

signpost
'Falling Foss'

SLEIGHTS road

A.169

road

700   600   500

above

178

lane road

gate

Chapel

Little Beck

BUTWARP road

ignore two paths branching left
spoil heaps (old quarry)

400   300

Nature Reserve

Little Beck

500   400

179

The Hermitage

157

THE HERMITAGE

The Hermitage

The Ordnance Survey maps are inconsistent in naming the hamlet 'Little Beck' (two words) on 2½" sheets and 'Littlebeck' (one word) on 1" sheets.

Top map revised 1994. For details of amended route, *see facing page.*

Falling Foss

THE HERMITAGE to GRAYSTONE HILLS

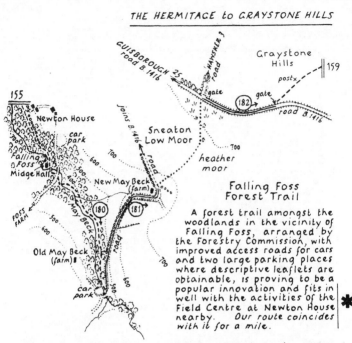

Falling Foss Forest Trail

A forest trail amongst the woodlands in the vicinity of Falling Foss, arranged by the Forestry Commission, with improved access roads for cars and two large parking places where descriptive leaflets are obtainable, is proving to be a popular innovation and fits in well with the activities of the Field Centre at Newton House nearby.   Our route coincides with it for a mile.

Without entering the grounds of Newton House, continue along a level path outside the estate wall, soon descending slightly to Falling Foss in surroundings of bewitching beauty. Pass in front of Midge Hall, now a museum, cross the wooden footbridge and walk upstream 70 yards to a stone bridge. Don't cross this but continue upstream following a direction sign to May Beck, on a path that crosses stepping-stones and goes on clearly with the stream on the right.   Disregard arrows on trees and a footbridge: these indicate the Forest Trail. The path finally emerges at the May Beck Car Park.   All this—path, car park and tarmac access road— is quite new within the past decade and a big surprise to anyone using old maps.   Go up the road, which overlooks the wooded valley just traversed, but beyond New May Beck Farm strike across the heather moor on the right to reach the busy road B.1416: the later stages of this crossing are swampy, but who cares about wet feet with Robin Hood's Bay only a few miles further? Now consult your watch.   A gated road, not signposted, going north from the B.1416 at the end of a plantation is much the quickest way to Hawsker, our next objective. The best way for lovers of heather moors with time to spare turns right along the B.1416, which happily has good wide verges and escapes from it at a gate on the left.

Map revised 1994 to show new route leading off the B1416.
*Newton House is no longer a Field Centre but a private residence.

According to the Ordnance maps, Craystone Hills is (or are) crossed by many footpaths and bridleways. But only the eye of faith can discern them on the ground, and, instead of wasting time searching for them, select the areas of moor with burnt or regenerated heather for the easiest walking. Aim slightly north of east at first, following grooves that suggest a former path of sorts, passing an old stone cross, which may not be noticed, and drawing near to the main Scarborough-Whitby road (A.171). At a gate in the fence a signpost gives the thrilling news that Robin Hood's Bay is only two miles distant along the facing side-road, and if it is wished to save time by avoiding the big detour to Hawsker you could be there, licking ice cream and eyeing the girls, in half an hour, mission accomplished.... But faithful followers of the recommended route will turn their face: to the moor again and, with the A.171 within shouting distance on the right, apply themselves to more trudging through the heather, now heading north. When a tumulus ahead makes a slight rise in the skyline keep left of it, reaching a tall gate in a fence, which climb (because it is padlocked) and go down rough ground to another gate giving access to a muddy lane that leads to a corner on a tarmac road. Here bear right for Hawsker, crossing the main road to the village street. Enough has now been done for the day and accommodation can be sought, but those who now really have the bit between their teeth and two hours of daylight left can push on along the road signposted to Robin Hood's Bay (2½ miles), keeping ahead when it curves to the right and following a lane past a caravan site and then crossing the track of the former railway. This latter, incidentally, gives a good fast walk to the Bay but like the tarmac road thereto is a temptation to be resisted. Such reluctance to take the quickest ways to the Bay is rather suggestive of a cat playing with a mouse before administering the coup de grâce, but the fact is that the royal road to the Bay undoubtedly is the coast path, pouncing on the prey from the top of the cliffs. That's the way we'll go, so carry on down the lane and don't argue.

Hawsker
(omitting the TV aerials but including the drainpipes)

*See note opposite

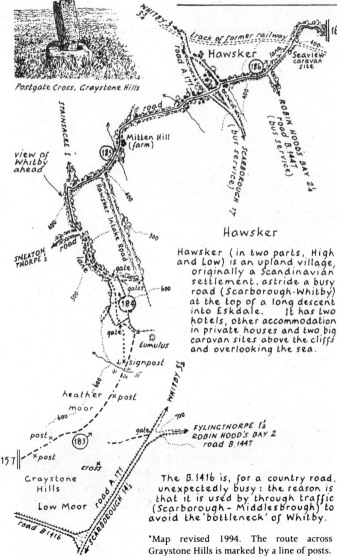

Postgate Cross, Graystone Hills

WHITBY 3¾

road A.171

Track of former railway

Hawsker

→ 161

Seaview
caravan
site

ROBIN HOOD'S BAY 2¼
road B.1447
(bus service)

186

road

STAINSACRE 1

Mitten Hill
(farm)

185

view of
Whitby
ahead

SCARBOROUGH 17
(bus service)

Hawsker Intake Road

road

SNEATON
THORPE 2

lane

400

500

500

gate

gates

600

184

gate

tumulus

signpost

WHITBY 3½

heather

moor

post

600

gate

700

FYLINGTHORPE 1½
ROBIN HOOD'S BAY 2
road B.1447

post

183

157

post

cross

Graystone
Hills

Low Moor

road A.171

SCARBOROUGH 14½

road B.1416

Hawsker

Hawsker (in two parts, High
and Low) is an upland village,
originally a Scandinavian
settlement, astride a busy
road (Scarborough-Whitby)
at the top of a long descent
into Eskdale.   It has two
hotels, other accommodation
in private houses and two big
caravan sites above the cliffs
and overlooking the sea.

The B.1416 is, for a country road,
unexpectedly busy: the reason is
that it is used by through traffic
(Scarborough - Middlesbrough) to
avoid the 'bottleneck' of Whitby.

*Map revised 1994. The route across
Graystone Hills is marked by a line of posts.

Maw Wyke Hole

Enter Northcliffe caravan site and go down its left-hand road to a continuing path with Oakham Beck on the left and water in great quantity palpably near ahead. The Coast Path is met at a signpost overlooking Maw Wyke Hole.   After a halt to savour the acute personal satisfaction of arrival at the edge of the North Sea follow the Coast Path to the right.   There is no difficulty of route-finding, the path being in popular use and part of the long-distance Cleveland Way.   Accompanying it throughout is a wire fence or stone wall, usually to seaward, and a dozen or more stiles have to be negotiated, some being a trial to tired limbs. The cliff scenery is excellent.   A first sighting of Robin Hood's Bay is eagerly awaited but delayed until Ness Point is finally rounded...... but then, suddenly, there it is. Now for the coup de grâce!

Robin Hood's Bay

NORTH SEA
at last

Maw Wyke
Hole

signpost
(Coast
Path)

WHITBY

Oakham Beck

187   ignore stile to cliffs
      (keep on land side of wall)

Northcliffe
caravan site

159

Hawsker
Bottoms   300

track of former railway (Whitby–Scarborough)   400

barley
field

highest
point   brambles

grooved path in bracken

188

300

200

barley
fields

Coastguard
Station   Ness
                 Point

189

South of
Ness Point
crude stiles give
place to kissing gates,
hinting that civilisation
is near. It is, and it takes
the form of an avenue of
modern villas, which could be
Suburbia anywhere, especially
with a name like Mount Pleasant
North. The real Robin Hood's Bay
is found by turning left down
Station Road past the car park.
A narrow street with flights of steps
for pedestrians now descends very
steeply into a picturesque huddle
of red-roofed buildings literally
perched on the edge of the sea.
Proceed with
decorum to
the bottom of
the hill, to the
limit of terra firma,
where the tarmac ends
at a shingly beach
and the sea. Go
forward and put
your boot in the
first salt-water
puddle. By
this ritual
you will have
completed a
walk from one side of
England to the other.

WHITBY 5½
HAWSKER 2
road B 1447

400

300

high water mark   low water mark

reefs

car
park
200

bus stand

FYLINGTHORPE ½
SCARBOROUGH 17
road B 1447

100
Kings Beck

Robin Hood's Bay

190

promenade
'The Quarterdeck'   Well, that's it!!

Robin Hood's Bay

Robin Hood's Bay, locally known as Bay Town or simply as The Bay, was an obscure fishing village and reputedly a haunt of smugglers until its unique situation, medieval atmosphere and picturesque appearance began to earn for it a secondary livelihood from visitors. Today it is a showplace for tourists, an itinerary 'must', but happily its quaint features have been preserved. The coast here, ribbed with sandstone reefs and rich in fossils, is geologically interesting, but it is the 'town', the amazing cluster of red-roofed buildings perched one above another, the labyrinth of passageways and steps, crowded into a breach in the cliffs with remarkable economy of space, a nest crammed tight, that attracts most attention. Happily too summer car traffic is halted at the top of the hill leading down to the shore: the narrow streets and alleys are pedestrian precincts. There are several shops and ample hotel and private cottage accommodation, with a Youth Hostel nearby. The railway has ceased to function but there are bus services to Whitby and Scarborough from the suburbia that has sprung up around the hinterland of the Bay.

Bay Town

The end of the road

Now you can rest on your laurels in the Bay Hotel with a pint, but (let there be no misunderstanding about this) you do so at your own expense. It's no use saying "charge it to Wainwright" as you did at the Border Hotel at Kirk Yetholm.   No, sonny, that game won't work here. Pay for your own. I'm skint.

INDEX TO PLACE-NAMES ON THE MAPS

This index lists only the place-names on the detailed route maps. Other references to these names, where they occur in the illustrations and notes accompanying the maps, will be found on the same or opposite page.

INDEX continued

INDEX continued

INDEX continued

INDEX continued

*There is one inadvertent
omission from the index
but this of no importance,
it being extremely unlikely
that any reader will wish
to refer to GREAT TONGUE
on page 31.*

Some Personal notes
in conclusion

I am beginning to have second thoughts about "official" long-distance footpaths. I am now not at all sure that they are wholly to be commended. Insofar as they get people into the fresh air, well and good, for urban existence today demands an occasional change of environment; insofar as they provide a challenge, well and good, for a life without challenges is tedious. But the wide publicity given to them brings disadvantages. The official blessing and opening of a long-distance path is headline news. The word goes forth and the world pulls on his boots.

The first of them, the Pennine Way, has already been so much used that it is fast losing its original appeal as a wilderness walk and becoming a too-popular parade. There are blazed tracks and litter where once there were neither. Some paths are so badly eroded that diversions have been necessary. Farmers along the route, faced with broken walls and straying stock, are being sorely tried. Sheep are crippling and choking themselves with broken glass and plastic bags. In time you won't need a map: just follow the trail of empty cans and orange peel.

most walkers still walk for walking's sake, because they like doing it; not as an opportunity for mischief. These are the goodies, the folk who really enjoy an escape to the quietness of the countryside and the hills, leave no traces of their passage and cause no trouble. But there are also the baddies, attracted by the publicity given to official footpaths but careless about the country code, inconsiderate of others, rebels against conventions and customs and decent behaviour and a general nuisance. These are the inexperienced, who cannot read a map, and the complete nogs who have never seen one. Official footpaths are menaced by such. The trouble is that officially prescribed routes cannot be selective of their users. They are open to all. They invite all. They are used by all.

You don't need to have an official route to get you out into the open air. You don't have to wait for the Countryside Commission to say 'O.K. you can go!' You don't have to follow the crowds. In this country there are thousands of long-distance routes for walkers that have never suffered an official blessing (and are all the better for that) and any walker with initiative can plan his own itineraries simply by linking the public rights of way recorded on current issues of the 1" Ordnance maps. There is positively no end to the routes that can be worked out. You may follow high-level tracks over the hills; or circuit mountain watersheds; or march the boundary of your county, or any other; or trace old drove roads; or go from point A to point B, whether A and B are castles, Roman camps, stone circles, or whatever; or visit your maiden aunt in Bognor; or cross the country on canal towpaths; or follow rivers from source to sea.

And all on foot, using rights of way, causing no trespass and needing no permissions. The map of England is an oyster very rich in pearls. Plan your own marathon and do something never done before, something you will enjoy, a route that will take you to places often read about but never yet seen. You will be on your own, unhampered by human beings en bloc, relying on your own resources to complete what you set out to do. Preferably go alone and do it off your own bat, for it is the solitary walker, always, who most closely identifies himself with his surroundings, who observes as he goes along, who really feels the satisfaction of achievement. If you must have a friend choose one who is quiet.

This is the sort of thing I set out to do in this book. In offering the idea of a coast to coast walk I am not contradicting myself at all — there is nothing official about it: it is an example of what might be done without any opening speeches and fanfares : a personal venture. I describe the route I planned and walked, and, for any who care to tread in my footsteps, directions are given — it's a good expedition although I say it myself : ideal for connoisseurs of fine scenery — but I would feel I had succeeded better in arousing interest for the planning of private long-distance walks if the book induced some readers to follow instead their own star and find their own rainbow's end.

In planning the walk I had four main objectives:

1: to avoid towns;
2: to link together three National Parks;
3: to keep to high ground wherever practicable;
4: to use only rights of way and areas of open access.

The first was easy, Richmond being the only town visited and that by design; the second ensured a high quality of scenery throughout; the third, a personal preference, was practicable except for the crossing of the Vale of Mowbray; the fourth I hope I observed everywhere.

It took me a year and it was a journey of delight. St. Bees Head, habitat of countless seabirds, was a splendid start; Lakeland as ever was a sweet foretaste of heaven; the Westmorland plateau was a joy to walk upon, as limestone always is; the Pennine crossing was wilderness tramping, grim yet relieved by the larks and curlews and ill-fated grouse; the old lead mines of Swaledale, ugly yet fascinating; the Vale of Mowbray, tranquillity profound; the grand heather moors of Cleveland and finally quaint Robin Hood's Bay, with the north sea stretching into infinity. You could not have a better-defined start and finish, each with the waves lapping your boots, and the inbetween was (with reservations about the Vale of Mowbray) an inspiring pageant of beauty and interest. I can say now that I have walked from one coast of England to the other. A year ago I couldn't have said this.

It is a walk I recommend, not necessarily to undertake in a single journey, but in parts as place, time and weather become convenient. But as I said before, vary it to suit yourself: you may for example prefer a more exciting traverse of Lakeland; or feel that Tan Hill would please you more than Keld (incidentally, it wouldn't) or, in a magnificent finale, take to the Lyke Wake Walk instead of the easier route I followed myself. But always keep to rights of way and, of course, travel every inch of the way on foot. Then, with me, you will be able to say you have walked across England.

A comparison with the Pennine Way is inevitable. The Pennine Way is far longer and a greater challenge to stamina, but most of it lies over dreary moorlands. The Coast to Coast Walk is, in my opinion, immeasurably superior in scenic qualities, although it has no Hadrian's Wall to stimulate the imagination. You enjoy the Pennine Way, if at all, because it satisfies an ambition and is a personal achievement; certainly not for its ravishing scenery. The Coast to Coast Walk is enjoyable for its beauty, for the dramatic variations of landscape and for its many interesting relics, some rooted in prehistory. The start and finish of the Pennine Way are arbitrary, those of the Coast to Coast Walk are exact. One has a certain grandeur, the other a succession of charms. The Pennine Way is masculine; the Coast to Coast Walk has feminine characteristics. If there happens to be something in your temperament that makes you like the ladies the odds are that you will prefer the C. to C. You may not meet any but you will

be reminded of them. On the PW
you never give them a thought
.... well, hardly ever.

I finished the Pennine Way with
relief, the Coast to Coast Walk with
regret. That's the difference.

AW

June 1972

Reader's
LOG
OF THE
JOURNEY

The remaining pages in this book are intended for the personal use of readers engaged on the walk.

The Log lists the various sections of the route, each providing a good day's walk and ending at a place where refreshment and accommodation are normally available.   Each section is subdivided into convenient parts for the use of those who cannot, or prefer not to, attempt the whole journey at one time; and for others who, because of disability, old age or infirmity, can only be 'half-day' or 'hour or two' walkers. For those who are 'supported' and victualled by friends with a car, intermediate points in each section where a car may wait are indicated.

A walker doing the full journey at one go will be interested in the subdivisions only for the purpose of halting to record times of arrival and departure.

The following symbols are used in the Log:

√ : point accessible by car

X : bus service

N.G.R. : National Grid Reference

Miles { S : in section
       { C : cumulative

Times { A : of arrival
       { D : of departure

Better fill this in before you start

THIS BOOK BELONGS TO

Name :

Address :

If found unattended and obviously lost *please* send it to the above address.

LOG OF THE JOURNEY

Date	Section	N.G.R.	Miles S	Miles C	Times A	Times D	Weather
	✓ St Bees (sea wall)	NX 960118	-	-			
	✓ Sandwith	NX 964148	$4\frac{3}{4}$	$4\frac{3}{4}$			
	✗ Cleator	NY 015135	$8\frac{3}{4}$	$8\frac{3}{4}$			
	Dent	NY 038130	$10\frac{3}{4}$	$10\frac{3}{4}$			
	✓ Kinniside Stone Circle	NY 060140	$12\frac{1}{4}$	$12\frac{3}{4}$			
	✓ Ennerdale Bridge	NY 069159	$14\frac{1}{4}$	$14\frac{1}{4}$			
	Low Gillerthwaite	NY 139141	$4\frac{3}{4}$	19			
	Black Sail Hut	NY 194124	$8\frac{3}{4}$	23			
	✓ Honister Pass	NY 225136	$11\frac{1}{4}$	$25\frac{1}{4}$			
	✗* Seatoller	NY 244138	13	$27\frac{1}{4}$			
	✗* Rosthwaite	NY 259148	$14\frac{1}{2}$	$28\frac{3}{4}$			
	Greenup Edge	NY 286106	$3\frac{3}{4}$	$32\frac{1}{4}$			
	Helm Crag	NY 328092	$7\frac{1}{4}$	36			
	✗ Grasmere	NY 337075	$9\frac{1}{4}$	38			
	Grisedale Tarn (outlet)	NY 351122	$13\frac{1}{4}$	42			
	✗* Patterdale	NY 398159	$17\frac{3}{4}$	$46\frac{1}{2}$			

Angle Tarn (inlet)	NY 417146	2	48½
Kidsty Pike	NY 448126	5	51½
✓ Burn Banks	NY 507161	11	57½
✓ Rosgill Bridge	NY 534165	13¼	59¾
X* Shap	NY 562154	16	62½
✓ Oddendale	NY 593134	2½	65
X* B.6260 road	NY 629100	7	69½
✓ Sunbiggin Tarn	NY 677078	11¼	73¾
Smardale Bridge	NY 721059	15½	78
✓ Waitby road	NY 748072	17½	80
X* Kirkby Stephen	NY 774087	20	82½
Nine Standards Rigg	NY 826061	5½	88
✓ Raven Seat	NY 862033	10	92½
X* Keld	NY 892011	12¾	95¼
Swinnergill Mines	NY 912012	1½	96¾
Blakethwaite Mill	NY 937018	3½	98¾
✓ Surrender Bridge	SD 989999	7½	102¾
X* Reeth	SE 038993	11¼	106½

*very infrequent in 1994

LOG OF THE JOURNEY continued

Date	Section	N.G.R.	Miles S	C	Times A	D	Weather
	Marrick Priory	SE 067978	2	108½			
	✓ Marrick	SE 076982	3	109½			
	✓ Marske	NZ 105007	5½	112			
	Whitcliffe Wood	NZ 145014	8½	115			
	X Richmond	NZ 171009	10½	117			
	✓ Colburn	SE 196991	3	120			
	X* Catterick Bridge	SE 228993	5½	122½			
	✓ Bolton-on-Swale	SE 251992	7½	124½			
	✓ Rawcar Bridge	SE 299988	11¼	128¼			
	✓ Streetlam	SE 310989	12¼	129¼			
	✓ Danby Wiske	SE 337986	14	131			
	X Oaktree Hill	SE 361988	16	133			
	✓ Long Lane	SE 389998	18¼	135¼			
	✓ East Harlsey road	NZ 418010	20½	137½			
	X* A.19 road	NZ 442012	22½	139½			
	X* Ingleby Cross	NZ 449007	23	140			